GREEK
MYTHS & LEGENDS

✳   ✳   ✳

First published in Great Britain by Brockhampton Press, a member of the Hodder Headline Group,
20 Bloomsbury Street, London WC1B 3QA.

Copyright © 1998 Brockhampton Press.

ISBN 1 86019 207 6

A copy of the CIP data is available from the British Library upon request.

Created and produced by Flame Tree Publishing, a part of The Foundry Creative Media Company Limited,
The Long House, Antrobus Road, Chiswick, London W4 5HY.

GREEK
MYTHS & LEGENDS

K. E. SULLIVAN

CONTENTS

❊   ❊   ❊

INTRODUCTION

Each form of worship that hath swayed
The life of man, and given it to grasp
The master-key of knowledge, reverence,
Enfolds some germ of goodness and of right;
Else never had the eager soul which loathes
The slothful down of pampered ignorance
Found in it even a moment's fitful rest.

HOMER

HE MYTHS AND LEGENDS OF GREECE have come to us across thousands of years of alteration and embellishment, communicated by speech, by gestures, by art and music, and eventually by the written word. They are the subjects of poetry and plays, which combine stories, legends, folktales and religious myths, so that the myths and legends as we know them today present a veritable feast of images, associations and meanings.

The Greek people called themselves Hellenes, and their country Hellas. Greek is the name given to them by the Romans. The Greeks lived not only in Greece, as we know it today, but all around the Mediterranean, in what today is called Turkey, their lands stretching as far south as the tip of Spain. Their civilization is the oldest we know of, stretching back to the Bronze Age, around 3000 BC. Our understanding of the Greeks and their civilization was widened by the discovery of the treasures at Mycenae, in the north-west of the Peloponnesus, where a new kingdom was created when Crete fell into decay. Mycenaean Greece, which lasted from about 1400 to 1150 BC, was characterized by massive palaces on rocky coasts, and mountain tops. They were a warring people, fighting for wealth among themselves. They left treasures such as gold daggers and cups, death-masks and weapons, and impressive tributes to the gods which were as detailed as they were magnificent. The Trojan War took place in this glorious age, and Troy was, according to legend, a rich and luxurious city on the Asian side of the sea that separates Europe from Asia. There is no doubt that Troy existed, and the legends of this time are steeped in both fact and fiction, intertwined so as to make the very best stories which cannot fail to intrigue and to suspend all disbelief.

The Greek Dark Ages ensued, from about 1100 to 700 BC, and they were marked by the collapse of the Mycenaean civilization, destroyed by barbarian tribes of the Roman empire. There was violence and looting, war and plundering, providing little inspiration for literature or for art, and while myths and legends were carried through these years, there was little embroidery to what existed. The bards continued the tradition of storytelling, and great comfort was garnered from the exciting tales of Ancient Greece, with its palaces and romances, adventures and intrigue. And then came the advent of classical Greece, from 600 to 300 BC, when city states took the place of kingdoms, ruled by dictators and infantry warfare. This was a sophisticated civilization, developed in the city states of the mainland, and in the islands nearby, but it too was short-lived, and the empire of the Persians, which had expanded

Opposite: The gods and goddesses were glamorous, passionate creatures, characterized by deep-seated jealousies, petty hatreds and desperate bids for revenge.

towards the Aegean Sea, conquered the Greeks of Asia Minor, taking their political freedom, their wealth and then their great wisdom. From this time, the leadership of the Greeks passed to the mainland, especially to Athens, where it remained until the conquests of Alexander.

But it was many years before the cultural and intellectual development of the Greek civilization that gods and goddesses ruled the imagination, that myths and legends were a vital part of everyday life, when poets and musicians and writers found endless inspiration in the stories of the past, which they embalmed and then allowed to permeate every aspect of their culture, their enlightenment.

For the Greeks had a unique and varied past, riddled with developments which today make them one of the most fascinating civilizations on earth. They were the fathers of democracy, of medicine and political and moral ideals, they were great philosophers and scientists, and much of mythology represents their quest to understand more clearly the nature of the earth and its occupants.

The most ancient Greeks were farmers, tending their land and their flocks, bringing forth wheat, grapes and olives. Olive oil was used in cooking, in bathing, and to provide the fuel for lights, and grapes were harvested for delicious wines that became a staple of the Greek diet. Goats and sheep were raised in rocky mountain pastures, and a Greek shepherd would live a lonely life with his flock. Life was difficult and unpredictable, and it is not surprising that the people were comforted by the myths and legends which gave meaning to the disasters which befell them, to the plagues and disease which robbed them of their crop, to the unruly weather which killed their harvest, to the whispers and mysterious movements of the grasses in the half-light, the babble of the springs which were answered at once by the wind in the trees. The world was alive with magic, and the Greeks drew consolation from naming it, and making it a part of their lives. It was soothing to think that sacrifice, that eternal praise of a god might bring forth good omens; like religion is and has always been, the faith and the belief in the gods of Greece offered hope where there would have been emptiness.

The gods and the goddess of Greece were worshipped by the Greeks as were the heroes and heroines which existed alongside them. The legends which were created around these great figures were a key part of daily life, and their reverential treatment has filtered through to the modern day. A great deal of superstition still surrounds the myths and legends of Greece, and while the stories are more often than not communicated for entertainment, for many, they still hold a grain of truth, a note of caution to mortals.

Myths were woven around historical fact, real people and placess and true events. In this form they are legends, exaggerated, surely, and distorted to make them tellable, more exciting, but created in order to convey the basic moral message of an event which has had some significance in the lives of those touched by it. There were folktales, too, which are tales of enchantment, deceit and trickery, in which heroes and heroines live alongside nymphs, talking animals, giants, monsters and witches. Folktales are based on magic, and used to explain phenomena which may otherwise, to a mind uneducated in science, be frightening, and inexplicable. Folktales provide

Opposite: Myths were woven around historical fact, real people and events and places that truly existed; they were exaggerated and distorted to make the stories more tellable.

explanations for the wind, the trees, the weather, for echoes, ghosts and seasons.

Religious myths are an essential part of most cultures, and the Greeks are no exception. They are the myths of philosophy, addressing matters which concern all of us. They relate to the conception of the world, to death and to living, to gods and to the state of godliness. They may deal with matters relating to a specific tribe, culture or people, making sense of rituals, superstitions and routines.

The Greeks were craftsmen, and the ritual of praying to gods was as important to them as it was to the lonely shepherd on his rocky outpost. Masons and potters, metal-workers and candle-makers, all prayed to their patron the god Hephaestus. If Hephaestus was not honoured, pots would break, metal would turn brittle, an avalanche would fall upon a hapless stone mason as he worked in the quarry. And so too did travellers pray to Poseidon and to the gods of the wind, who could suddenly produce a storm that would wreck the vessel of even the most devout mortal.

It is easy to see how the myths and legends of Greece could be nurtured, could feed the collective imagination to such an extent that they have been expanded, cosseted and preserved by centuries of genius and artistic endeavour, passing into literature of other cultures and lands, where they are as enriching as they have been enriched. Their paganism had sprouted from some seed of believable notion, and while the stories have passed now into the realms of entertainment, they once held the greatest fascination and importance to their owners.

The myths and legends of Greece have come down to us through their great writers, who based their works on stories which have been told and retold for thousands of years. In Greece, before the advent of archaeology, the primary source of knowledge about their people and civilization was the poems of Homer, to which were attached a series of epics dealing with the Trojan War. *The Iliad*, for example, relates to events which occurred in the tenth year of that war. The journey of the Odysseus, in *The Odyssey*, tells the tale of his return home to Ithaca. Homer describes the part played by Greek gods on the way, who fought on one side or another, depending on who was in favour.

After Homer came Hesiod, who attempted to put together the pieces of the war in a more comprehensive form, in his *Works and Days* and *Homeric Hymns*. These were intended, in the form of poetry, to link Greek families to the gods through their genealogical trees. The Theogony is the account of the gods and heroes, and their struggle with the giants at the beginning of time. And then came storytellers, who sought to put in narrative the most evocative of the legends, and those which provided the most significance to daily life. Hecataetus of Miletus is one such story-teller, and it was he who said, 'The stories the Greeks tell are many and, in my opinion, ridiculous. What I write is what I believe to be true.'

Hecataetus attempted to give a reasoned explanation for the creation of the earth, and for ensuing events, and it was this prying into nature which led to the birth of modern philosophy. But the Greeks were not as eager to lose their heritage, and believed firmly in the existence of their gods and heroes, through mythology, long after the death of Hecataetus.

Some areas of Greece were richer sources of legends than others, including Argolis, Boeotia, Thessaly and Attica. Some legends were local, and others extended to encompass the whole of the classical world, eventually translated into Latin by the Romans when they took over the empire. Legends which spread far and wide include the myths of Heracles, Jason and the Argonauts, and Odysseus. Others became the subjects of Greek literature, in particular plays and epic poems which were recited to large audiences by the rhapsodes, the succours of the bard who sang and played at Homeric feasts. Concerts for playwrights and rhapsodes were held at Epidars, a theatre built in the fourth century BC, which seated up to 14,000 people. Authors like Sophocles and Euripides altered the legends, creating endings or diversions that would appeal to a more modern audience.

But for many Greeks, Homer was their bible, and school-children, once education was made possible, grew up using *The Iliad* and *The Odyssey* as their textbooks. And today they hold an important place in the study of history and of

Opposite: Poseidon ruled the sea with a will of iron. He dictated the currents, the waves and the direction of the rivers and streams, and he was often unpredictable, impetuous and unkind.

literature, and it is impossible, sometimes, to see them as more than that, to understand what they really meant to the Greeks and their civilization. Our knowledge of myths is of course mainly through their literature, which is made more real by their art, and given credibility by architectural discoveries. We know there are many myths which have been lost, referred to in other works, and that many lyrical poets have cut or destroyed whole swathes of their work, for many great narrative poems fail to tell a story in a linear sequence. Great historians, like Euhemerus, in the fourth century, reinterpreted the myths, believing them to be based on great men of the past, not deities.

Apollodorus, in the second century, provided us with an indispensable encyclopaedia of mythology, and his work is a scholarly attempt to make sense of a plethora of gods and kings, all of whom appeared to live simultaneously, or with huge gaps between their reigns. Alexandrian poetry traced myths still further, and poets like Theocritus or Callimauchus narrated myths which are new, perhaps to them, or just retold versions of a theme which had not been recorded earlier. Later scholars refused to discard the rich tradition of myths as nonsense, or indeed entirely as fiction. Strabo, for instance, in his introduction to *Geography*, called the study of Greek myths essential to the understanding of history and ultimately philosophy. He felt that myths were a palliative which allowed knowledge to be absorbed and carried on, presenting facts interspersed with clever fiction, almost novel-like in their importance and accuracy. Plutarch, in the second century AD, called mythology a kind of warped religion, 'reflections of some true tale which turns back our thoughts to other matters'.

The Romans leapt upon the pantheon of Greek gods with a vengeance, and they became even further ingrained in the consciousness of the European culture, which eventually spread northwards and across the oceans. Ovid and Virgil gave the myths new meaning and significance, imbibing them with credibility and elevating them to an art form. And with each ensuing generation, writers and readers have been inspired by the myths of the Greeks, and have adopted them as an essential part of their culture, retold, reworked and often redesigned for a new audience, but most importantly continued.

But bearing in mind the importance of the role of myths in the lives of the Greeks, it is essential that their motivation for creating them is understood. The Greeks created myths in order to make a pronouncement, to say something about their experience of the world. The fact that they have passed into ours is indicative of the infallibility of their myths to enchant, to please, and to offer answers to some of the eternal questions, whether or not we choose to believe them.

Many of the earliest legends deal with the concept of chaos, a state which existed before the beginning of the world. This emphasis on religious or philosophical interpretation of the evolution of the earth is not unique to the Greeks – most cultures and civilizations have their own answers to the questions that have plagued mankind from the beginning of time. But the Greeks believed that from chaos was born the goddess Gaea or Ge, called 'Wide blossomed Earth, the sure foundation of all, the eldest of beings who supports creatures and things.' And it is here that the story begins, the consummation of divine forces which conceived everything around us, the birthplace of earth. The beginning of time was created and peopled by gods, and these were the threads of some of the greatest myths and legends of all time. They are a part of our world, a part of our culture, our fundamental beliefs and our understanding of ourselves and each other. The Greek gods and heroes have never failed to captivate, and their importance cannot be overstated.

Opposite: Apollo was the son of Zeus and Leto, and the god of plague, music, song and prophecy. He was the twin of Artemis and both lived on Mount Olympus in all the splendour of the gods

The Pantheon

AFTER EARTH CAME EROS, who was not the god of love (Cupid) as he became known in later legends, but an immortal being who rose to send passion to earth, which would eventually govern the hearts of men and gods. From chaos came Darkness and Night, called Erebus and Nyx, and these drew together to create Aether, the air, and Hemera, the day. This was light, and the beginning of our world as we know it.

Then Ge, or Gaea spawned Uranus, the starry heaven, who became her partner. Other deities were spat out of chaos, including Doom, Black Fate, Sleep, Death and Woe, then the Hesperides who guard the apples on the edge of the Western world, Destiny and Fate, and then Nemesis, Deceit, Age, Strife and Friendship. From Uranus and Ge, was born the first race of divine children, twelve of them known as the Titans. One of them, Rhea, replaced her mother as Earth goddess, and Cronus would take over the role of his father Uranus. Oceanus was also born of Uranus and Ge, and he was the father of many, including Nereus, the Old Man of the Sea.

These were the forefathers of many great heroes and gods, including Achilles and Iris.

The Titans were despised by Uranus, who jealously believed that they wished to destroy him. They were hidden underground by their mother, from where they were eventually liberated by Cronus, who made his father impotent. One night he took the sickle of Ge, and waited in ambush for his father. He reached out and castrated Uranus, flinging his genitals out to the sea. There they touched the foam and from it sprung the goddess Aphrodite, who rose of the sea to the island of Cythera. There she was joined by Eros and Desire, and the three immortals, and they lived there together, putting together their powers in order to plague the hearts of mortals with their actions. When drops of his blood touched the ground, giants sprang forth, along with nymphs called the Meliai, and the avenging Furies. Cronus took over the rule from his father, and the first generation of gods was now in place.

Cronus and Rhea married, but before their first child could be born, Cronus was told by an Oracle that he would be supplanted by one of his sons. In response, he devoured each child as it was born, eating Poseidon, Demeter and Hera, Hestia and Hades in this way. Rhea was filled with grief, and as each child was snatched from her she grew more rebellious, more angry. She begged her parents for help, and when she was heavy with Zeus, she was spirited off into the night by Ge, who allowed the baby to be born in the safety of Lyktos in Crete. Zeus was hidden in a cave, and Rhea wrapped a large boulder in swaddling clothes, which she presented to her husband instead. The boulder was swallowed whole, and Zeus was saved. He was brought up by Ge, fed on the milk of goats and on nectar and honey, and the nymphs of the mountains guarded over him, taking great pleasure in their important role.

The sands of time slipped by, bringing with them manhood for Zeus, who as he grew vowed revenge on his father. With the help of Metis, the daughter of Oceanus, he presented Cronus

Opposite: The Muses were the goddesses of poetry and song, the daughters of Zeus and Mnemosyne. They lived on Mount Helicon and inspired gods and mortals alike

with a draught which caused him to vomit up his children. From Tartarus, Zeus also released the giants and Cyclopes born of Ge, and he enlisted their help in overthrowing his father. The Cyclopes were so grateful for their freedom that they presented Zeus with thunderbolts and lightning, with which he could do battle. And so it came to pass that these creatures were gods, and went to live on Mount Olympus, where they enraged the Titans, with the exception of Oceanus, who swore revenge against them.

The Titans lived on Mount Othrys, and from there they launched attacks on Mount Olympus, and so commenced a war that lasted ten bloody years, as the earth was ravished and ravaged by battle. It was won at last by the gods, and the Titans were cast deep into the bowels of the earth.

But in the tumultuous new world, where order had not yet cast a cloak of calm, war followed war, and the next threat to the gods was the attack of the giants who had been born from the blood of Uranus. They attacked Olympus, almost scaling its heights before Zeus, with the aid of Heracles, cast them aside. Then Ge, distraught by the plight of her children, sent a monster, Typhon, to fight Zeus, but it too was beaten by the powerful thunderbolts of the king of gods, and it fled to Mount Etna, where it took refuge in its base.

And the world shook and twisted, all at once turbulence and misfortune. Volcanoes erupted, earthquakes and tornadoes broke and churned the earth's surface. Whirlpools thrust themselves up from the great boiling sea, and then, when the final war was waged, all was quiet. The birds flew tentatively from their nests, animals and trees poked their heads above the earth, which blossomed once more, flowering with peace and new hope. There was tranquillity across the lands, and to the top of Mount Olympus went Zeus and his gods, where they built their thrones. There they lived in luxurious palaces, guardians of the mortals who went about their humble duties on the earth. From their supernatural realm they toyed with the lives of men on earth, occasionally intervening, often falling in love with their playthings, demanding sacrifices and holy worship, sitting back on their opulent thrones drinking nectar, and feeding on ambrosia.

Mount Olympus sits on the border between Macedonia and Thessaly, the towering pinnacle some 9500 feet in height. Its tip is wreathed in cloud, enshrouding the immortals from the prying gazes of men. Their palaces were the stuff of dreams, cast in gold and marble, encrusted with jewels and hung with fine fabrics. Music was piped through heated rooms, where gods and

goddesses bathed, and feasted, and lolled in complete comfort. They dabbled in the events on earth beneath them, and although they found themselves victims, instigators and pawns in war, they could not be killed, for instead of true blood, ichor ran through their noble veins.

There were twelve gods on the mountain of Olympus, and they were headed by Zeus, thunderer and lord of the Bright sky. He was the chief of gods, their king, and he was honoured with many names. His brothers were Poseidon and Hades, but the latter did not live on the mountain, but beneath the earth in the Underworld, where he was king. Many years before Zeus came to power, the three godly brothers had drawn straws to divide the ancestral estate of Cronus and Rhea. Poseidon had drawn the sea, Zeus the heavens, and Hades the world below, and although they shared the job of governing the earth and everything above and beneath it, Zeus was the mightiest, and the most divine.

Zeus was a lusty god, and he was not content with just one partner in his bed. He slept with Themis, who gave birth to Eunomia, Dice and Eirene, also known as Government, Justice and Peace. And then Eurynome spawned the Graces. Next Demeter shared his bed, and Persephone was their offspring, who later became her uncle's queen. Mnemosyne and Zeus produced the nine Muses, and Leto bore him the twins Apollo and Artemis. Finally Zeus chose as his wife Hera, and she became the queen of Olympus, but he was not monogamous, and many more children were born to him, including Hermes, the divine messenger, Dionysus, the god of wine, and from Hera herself were produced Ares, Hebe and Eileithyia, the god of war, the goddess of youth, and the goddess of childbirth.

Zeus's brother Poseidon ruled the sea with a will of iron, and he was also master of horses, riding a chariot drawn by splendid steeds. When he travelled by sea, his chariot was pulled by Tritons, who were half men, half fish. His palace lay beneath the fiery sea, a sumptuous castle which glittered through the waves, seen for a splendid instant and then gone again, almost entirely invisible to enquiring eyes. He dictated the currents, the waves and the direction of the rivers and streams, and he was often unpredictable, impetuous, and unkind. He brought fear to the heart of mortals for he was easily upset, and difficult to placate. He married Amphitrite, a jealous and vengeful wife, but he too laid with many others, fathering Pegasus, Arion and the Mysteries.

Hades ruled the Underworld with wisdom, and he grew to love the deep, dark and forbidding place from which no mortal could return. He was called Zeus of the Underworld, and he was a severe and uncompromising leader, who provided the punishments decreed by his brother Zeus. His chariot was drawn by black horses which came to embody anarchy and destruction, controlled only by their tempestuous leader. When he left his kingdom he often travelled in the cloak of invisibility, surprising mortals by his sudden appearance, and thereby becoming a presence to be feared. He was a rich god, owner of all the jewels and metals in the earth, and he had a deep knowledge of the ill deeds of men, which caused him to be called the good counsellor.

Other gods and goddesses on Mount Olympus included Hephaestus, Hermes, Ares, Apollo, Hera, Athene, Artemis, Hestia, Aphrodite and Demeter. There were other deities including Helius (god of the sun), Selene (goddess of the moon), Leto, Dionysus and Themis. Those who waited on the gods lived there as well, and they were the messenger Iris, Hebe, who served them their food and drink, the Graces, the Muses and Ganymedes, the cup-bearer.

For many millennia these gods ruled the earth, until the time came for Dionysius to take over the reins, at which the kingdom of Zeus passed away. And in that time, the world came also to be populated by mortals, of whom there were five ages. The first was the Golden Age, when man was free from toil and illness, described by Hesiod in his *Works and Days*:

Like gods they lived, with calm untroubled mind,
Free from the toil and anguish of our kind:
Nor e'er decrepit age mis-shaped their frame,
The hand's, the foot's proportions, still the same.
Pleased with the earth's unbought feasts, all ills removed,
Wealthy in flocks, and of the bless'd beloved,
Death as a slumber pressed their eyelids down;
All nature's common blessings were their own;
The life-bestowing tilth its fruitage bore,
A full, spontaneous and ungrudging store:
They with abundant goods, mid quiet lands,
All willing shared the gathering of their hands.

The Golden Age was followed by the Age of Silver, when man was less noble, and incurred more often the wrath of the gods. The Bronze Age brought man who insisted on fighting with weapons made of bronze, and this race was, like the one before it, destroyed by the angry gods, who had not been appeased or pandered to. The fourth age brought Iron. It was an age of heroes and demi-gods, many of whom were killed in battle and in war. This was the time of the Trojan War and a time when man as we know it was evolving from the grandeur of his ancestors, many of whom lived on that great mount of Olympus.

And then the fifth age is ours, a time when, as Hesiod says,

Far-seeing Zeus made yet another generation of men, who are upon the bounteous earth ... and men shall never rest from labour and sorrow by day, and from perishing by night, and the gods shall lay sore trouble on them ... Strength will be right and reverence shall cease to be; and the wicked will hurt and ... man, speaking false words against him ...

If his words are prophecy, then our lives are still governed by those passionate gods, high on the mountain of Olympus. The following presents a picture of some of these deities, and these are their stories.

✱   ✱   ✱

AUTHOR'S NOTE

The plethora of myths and the variety of interpretations between them dictate that many of the most memorable of the Greek myths and legends cannot be included in this collection. Heroes like Heracles, Achilles and Jason, for example, are the subjects of dozens of myths across the centuries, but the scope of this book would not allow the inclusion of every great story. Instead you will find here a selection of evocative and enchanting myths and legends, most well-known, and all of which have left a lasting impression on our culture. They are often a combination of several versions, including those of Homer, Ovid, and more recently, Robert Graves and A.R. Hope Moncrieff. The author acknowledges their essential contribution to what follows.

TALES OF TROY

he city of Troy grew on the low hill on the plain near the entrance to the Hellespont, founded by Ilus, a descendant of Zeus, who marked out the boundaries of a city and settled there. Ilus prayed to the gods for good luck and discovered the following morning a large wooden statue, the Palladium, the image that the goddess Athene had made in memory of her friend Pallas. Apollo appeared and begged Ilus to keep sacred the image, to guard and respect it against all invaders. As long as Troy preserved the token of godly esteem, the city would be safe. But men being men, and even then subject to the fates and powers of the gods, events would occur to threaten the sanctity of the beautiful city of Troy. And that city would become the food of legends for aeons to come, the site of a battle which involved the greatest heroes of Greece, the most powerful gods of Olympia, and the most beautiful women in the land. The tales of Troy are the longest and most exciting of all the legends, and they begin with a beautiful woman, and a handsome man, cast from his noble birth ...

The Judgement of Paris

THE GOOD NAME OF TROY had been blackened over the years by many of the gods, who had been wronged by her leaders. These gods held a grudge that was relaxed only under the shrewd and swift-footed King Priam, who took over the reins of Troy and allowed her once more to blossom. Now Priam was a superstitious and careful monarch, never erring in order that his command of the lovely land might be released. And when his wise wife Hecuba dreamed that she had borne a firebrand their youngest son was cast away, left to die on the heights of Mount Ida.

This child was Paris, but he did not die. He was suckled by a bear and brought to live with the herdsmen of the mountain, where he grew strong and handsome, proud and respected by his peers. He grew up ignorant of his noble breeding, content to wed and live with an exquisite mountain nymph Oenone in a humble home. He was called Alexander there, the 'helper of men'.

And then one day, as he tended his flocks on the sunlit mountains, surrounded by greenery, and more than content with his simple lot, he was visited by Hermes, messenger of the gods. There had been an altercation he said, looking with awe at the beauty of this mortal, and three of the loveliest goddesses required a judge to ascertain which was the fairest. It had been decreed by Zeus that Paris was a man of great wisdom and fair looks, and that this lowly shepherd should be given the task of judging amongst the goddesses.

'Fear not, Paris,' said Hermes, 'Zeus bids thee judge freely which of the three seems fairest in thine eyes; and the father of gods and men will be thy shield in giving true judgement.'

Paris nodded in amazement, the sanctity of his simple life at once eclipsed by the excitement and shallowness of the deed before him.

The first goddess to appear to him was Hera, Queen of Olympus. She explained to the young shepherd that a wedding had taken place between Peleus and Thetis, to which Eris alone among the immortals had not been included through some oversight. She had appeared nonetheless at the feast, and churning trouble, she threw an apple at the feet of three of the greatest of the goddesses, those who thought themselves the most beautiful in the land – Hera, Athene and Aphrodite. The apple was inscribed with the words: *For the Fairest*.

Opposite: Aphrodite was as beautiful as her sisters but with a cunning that matched her looks.

'I am Aphrodite,' she said softly, coyly.

And it was to judge that fairest that Paris had been summoned, to put an end to the petty quarrelling. Hera went on to offer him all her queenly gifts, including money and the richest land on earth.

Athene offered him wisdom and success in battle, 'Adjudge the prize to me,' she whispered, 'and thou shall be famed as the wisest and bravest among men.'

The third goddess was Aphrodite, as beautiful certainly as her sisters, but with cunning that matched her looks. 'I am Aphrodite,' she said softly, coyly drawing herself up to the shepherd. 'I can offer thee gifts that are sweeter than any on earth. He who wins my favour needs only love to be loved again. Choose me, and I promise thee the most beautiful daughter of men to be thy wife.'

And although Paris was wed already, he chose Aphrodite without a moment's hesitation, and he gave the golden appple to the goddess of love who thanked him with such a radiant smile that his cheeks were rouged with pleasure.

It was with this glow of gratification that Paris set off the next day to take part in the games arranged each year by King Priam to commemorate the death of his youngest son, Paris. It was his first visit to the city since his birth, and he was anxious to test his strength. He excelled at the games, his strength, his passion and his ambition surpassing even that of his own brothers, the young princes of Troy. And when they, greatly angered by his prowess, took offence, and plotted to have an errant arrow sent in his direction, his sister Cassandra, who had a gift of divination, shouted out, not knowing what she said, 'Do not raise your hand against your brother.'

The princes were aghast, King Priam delighted, and it was with open arms that Paris was reunited with his family and welcomed back to Troy. He was given a great duty to perform for the King, to travel to Greece in order to secure the return of Hesione who had been borne off by Hercules many years before. Cassandra alone was vehemently against this venture, her prophetic vision showing her death and destruction that would lead to a great war against Troy. But her words were ignored, and Paris set off on his voyage, stopping during its course to visit Menelaus, king of Sparta, who was married to Helen, the most beautiful woman in the world.

It was this diversion which led Helen far from her marriage vows, into the arms of another man in an elopement which would excite the world of Greece and begin a battle that would run for ten long, blood-thirsty years.

Helen and Paris

The face that launched a thousand ships,
And burnt the topless towers of Ilium.

HOMER

HELEN WAS THE DAUGHTER of Leda and Tyndareus, King of Sparta, and she was undoubtedly the most beautiful woman in all of Greece. Her beauty caused her to be carried off to Attica by Theseus, and to be worshipped as a goddess at Sparta. As she grew older, she attracted suitors from around the world who swarmed to her side in order that she might receive their attentions.

Men with impeccable records of bravery, with inordinate riches, vied to become Helen's husband, including the wise and cunning Odysseus, Ajax, Diomedes, Philoctetes and Menestheus. Tyndareus did not wish to offend these great men, and he chose the wealthiest of the princes, Menelaus, brother of Agamemnon, lord of Argos, who was married to Helen's half-sister Clytemnestra. Odysseus suggested to Tyndareus that the suitors who had not been chosen to wed Helen should take a vow, swearing to defend to the death the lucky suitor, should anyone or anything appear to strip him of his good fortune. And so it was that Menelaus became King of Sparta, married to the exquisite Helen, who lived with him in harmony and happiness. He was warmly congratulated by the suitors who had not been chosen, and bound by their vow, they returned to their respective homes. Tyndareus marked the occasion by providing an offering to the gods, but it was ill fortune indeed that he omitted Aphrodite in his address, an oversight that would be long remembered and regretted by mortals and gods alike.

Helen gave birth to three children, and all was well in the luxurious palace, where food and drink were plentiful, where Menelaus ruled fairly and kindly, and where Helen and Menelaus grew to find a mutual respect and adoration for one another.

And then, one cruel day, the Fates chose to send to Sparta the ship of Paris, who decided, from the moment he set eyes on Helen, that he must have her as his wife. His true wife Oenone was forgotten, lonely on the Mount of Ida, and so too were his sense of honour, his mission, and the commands of his long-lost father. He called to Aphrodite to fulfil the promise she had made to him on the hillside, and when honest Menelaus set out on an expedition, he trusted the lovesick Paris to care for his wife in a

manner befitting his status. Before he could return, Paris had eloped with Helen leaving behind Hermione, her daughter by Menelaus.

With treasure they had looted from the palace of Menelaus, Paris and Helen sailed idly, deep in love that blossomed as they travelled. It was only after months of tender lovemaking, and a true, rich affection, that Paris returned home to Troy, to show off his prize. On their journey, however, the sea became suddenly calm, no breath of air rippling her surface. An eerie silence fell upon them, threatened to overwhelm them with its sinister threat of ill-fate. And then, from the sea, rose a creature so fearful, that Paris thrust Helen below the deck, and with his sword ready, moved forward to hear its words. The quiet was deafening. The creature spoke not, but laid its dripping trident across the prow of the ship and leant forward, its mighty weight dipping the vessel dangerously close to the edge of the sea. And then it uttered words that chilled the heart of Paris.

'I am Nereus, god of the sea. Ill omens guide thy course, robber of another's goods. The Greeks will come across this sea, vowed to redress the wrong done by thee and to overthrow the towers of Priam. How many men, how many horses I see there, dead for thy misdeed, how many Trojans murdered for thy sins, how many Trojans laid low about the ruin of their city!' And with that he cast his trident high into the sky, and disappeared beneath the mirrored sea.

But the deed was done, and fate had cast the die. Paris had been weak in mind and body, and for those sins he would bring about the disgrace and disintegration of Troy and her people. Head down, he surged across the waves that swelled up to greet them, breathed in the air that began to circulate once more. In the name of love, and on the wings of pride, he continued on to Troy, determined to build a life there with his lady love.

The Seeds of War

THE ELOPEMENT OF PARIS and Helen sent waves of shock through the land. Menelaus, his trusting soul rent by sadness, gathered together those men who had pledged an oath to aid him in times of trouble. He called upon all the great rulers from other lands, men who would take up their arms to recover his beloved wife, and to punish the violator of his home. He and his brother Agamemnon were the greatest and most powerful lords of the Peloponnese, and together they summoned the

Opposite: Paris eloped with Helen, leaving behind Hermione and all that she had grown to love at Troy. They sailed idly, deep in a love that blossomed as they travelled.

finest leaders of the land to bring their ships and their most courageous war-riors for war against Troy, and ever respectful of these two great men, all but two answered the call and set out for Troy.

One of these men was Odysseus, a crafty and highly regarded leader of the small island of Ithaca. Odysseus had recently married his great love Penelope, who had given birth to their son Telemachus. He had found great happiness with his family, and was loath to quit it for a war which had been predicted as long and painful. An Oracle had confirmed to him that he risked twenty years of separation from his home and his wife if he travelled to Troy, and he was not inclined to respond to the summons. Instead, he feigned madness, and when he was visited in person by Menelaus and Palamedes, he put on a rustic cap and ploughed salt into the furrows of his rocky land, with an ox and an ass yoked together. But Palamedes was not fooled by this show, and he laid down the infant Telemachus, in the path of the plough, at which Odysseus was forced to admit his deceit, pull up the team, and rescue his son from certain danger. And so it was that Odysseus travelled reluctantly to Troy, where the oracle proved true, but where he made his name as the most distinguished warrior of all time.

Achilles was also summoned, but had defied the call on the advice of his mother Thetis, who had dressed him in the garb of a maiden and hid-den him among the daughters of the King of Scyros. He was the son of Peleus, a mortal who had married the goddess Thetis. Achilles was the youngest of many children born to Thetis, but all had died as she attempted to immortalize them by holding them over a fire. When Achilles was born, she wished once more to make him immortal, but cleverly ignored the murderous flames which promised such status and hung him instead over the waters of the River Styx, making him invulnerable by dipping him into the waters. The heel by which she held him remained the one vulnerable part of his body, and he was brought up with other heroes by Cherion, who fed him on the hearts of lions and the marrow of bears. He was a popular boy, endowed with great prowess and skill in war.

Opposite: The walls of Troy had been built by Apollo and Poseidon themselves, and could not be damaged or scaled, despite the best efforts of Aganamemmon's army, so the city was held in siege, cut off from the outside world for ten long years.

His mother knew that the Trojan war would lead to his certain death, and it was she who hatched the plan to hide him from Menelaus and his men. But it was crafty Odysseus who found him, and revealed him by disguising himself as a purveyor of fine fabrics and jewellery, which provided great excitement to the other young women, but which failed to interest the young hero. When cunning Odysseus laid out a dagger and shield they were leapt upon by

Achilles, who disclosed himself, and came readily with Odysseus.

When King Priam heard news of Paris's activities at Sparta, he sank back in disbelief. Odysseus had journeyed to Troy with Palamedes and Menelaus, to demand that Priam return Helen, but Paris had not yet returned to the island and Priam was loath to judge a man before he'd had his say. He responded with courtesy to the requests of these great men who had appeared on his shores with such an urgent mission, but he put them off. And when Paris did finally appear with Helen, King Priam and his sons were so besotted by her, so taken by her beauty that they forgave Paris all his weakness and swore that Helen should remain in Troy for ever. Helen confirmed that she had eloped of her own free will, and that her love for Paris was greater than any known to man or god before them.

However, the people of Troy were less kindly disposed to their new mistress, for with her she brought the threat of war, which would draw into action its many men, and rob them of their freedom and good name. And when Paris stalked the streets of Troy, his new bride on his arm, he was followed by muttered curses. The men of Troy gathered together their troops, led by the great Hector, and Priam's son-in-law, Aeneas, prince of the Dardinians and son of Aphrodite herself.

Many years had passed since Menelaus had put out that first call for assistance, but the impressive collection of warriors grouped now at Aulis, a harbour on the Ruipus, where more than a thousand ships were gathered. But as they prepared to set forth for Troy, their sails were met by calm that disallowed even a breath of wind to set them on their course. And so it transpired that Artemis was behind the deathly stillness, for Agamemnon had unwittingly hurt her pride by slaying one of her sacred hind, and she now demanded the death of Agamemnon's own daughter Iphigenia in return.

Agamemnon was torn by the command and refused to consider it, while the men of Greece became surly and impatient to begin a war which threatened to be long and hard. So the great lord listened to his men, and encouraged by his brother Menelaus, he called his wife to bring Iphigenia to the site, where he promised her Achilles as a husband. And for that reason alone, Iphigenia was brought to the ships, and when she greeted her father with excitement and love, he cast her aside, daring not to meet her glances. Seeing his unhappiness, Menelaus swallowed his own sadness and forbade his brother to kill the young girl, but this sympathy and pity hardened the heart of Agamemnon and he prepared for the sacrifice.

Opposite: Odysseus put on a rustic cap and ploughed salt into the furrows of his rocky land, with an ox and an ass yoked together.

Clytemnestra was Agamemnon's wife, and she grew suspicious when she saw him shirk the embraces of his favourite daughter. She took herself to the tent of Achilles, who professed no knowledge of an impending wedding, and finally admitted the real purpose of Iphigenia's visit to the camp. In a fiery rage and distress, Clytemnestra flew back to her husband, and found her daughter begging for mercy at his feet.

And then, as Agamemnon struggled again to make a decision that would calm his angry men, console his desperate wife, Iphigenia drew herself up, and wiping away her tears, proclaimed, 'Since so it must be, I am willing to die; then shall I be called the honour of Greek maidenhood, who have given my life for the motherland. Let the fall of Troy be my marriage feast, and my monument.' And the brave young woman cast herself down on the sacrificial table at the altar of Artemis, gazing heavenward as her peaceful expression filled her family with woe anew.

The seer Calchas unsheathed the knife, having been given this painful duty, but as he lifted his arm to strike a blow, Iphigenia vanished, taken by Artemis herself who had pitied the lovely maiden, and borne her away to become a priestess of her temple at Tauris, to live in eternal maidenhood. In her place on the table lay a snow-white fawn, sprinkled with virgin blood, and with a great roar of gladness, Calchas proclaimed Artemis to be appeased. His words were carried away on the whisper of wind that grew until it became a mighty gale, pulling at the idle ships and filling her crew with anticipation and joy.

The winds carried them to Lesbos, and then on to the island of Tenedos, from where the distant walls of Troy could be seen glowing in the light of dawn. The war would begin.

The Trojan War

Many a fire before them blazed:
As when in heaven the stars about the moon
Look beautiful, when all the winds are laid
And every height comes out, and jutting peak
And valley, and the immeasurable heavens
Break open to their highest, and all the stars
Shine, and the Shepherd gladdens in his heart:
So many a fire between the ships and stream
Of Xanthus blazed before the towers of Troy,
A thousand on the plain; and close by each
Sat fifty in the blaze of burning fire;
And champing golden grain the horses stood
Hard by their chariots waiting for the dawn.

ALFRED, LORD TENNYSON

THE WAR BEGAN BADLY, with the death of Tenes, the son of Apollo, before the invaders had reached the shores of Troy. Achilles had been warned never to take the life of any child of Apollo, but when he saw a figure hurling rocks at the ships of the Greeks, who were approaching the walled city of Troy, he struck him down with one swoop of his mighty sword. Tenes was dead before Achilles could be cautioned, and gloom was cast over the ships as they waited warily for Apollo to strike his revenge.

Then the excellent marksman Philtoctetes was bitten by a snake, causing a wound so stagnant with infection that the Greeks had no choice but to leave the warrior on the rocky island off Lemnos, where he was abandoned and forced to live alone for many years. And while the sombre army struggled to come to terms with the loss of one of their greatest men, Protesilaus, a youth of determination and valour, leapt on to the beaches of Troy where he was slain instantly by Troy's champion Hector, Priam's eldest son. The war had begun. It had been decreed by Zeus himself that mankind must be depleted, and so it was that the gods themselves became involved in a war that had been sparked by one single mortal woman.

Opposite: Achilles and his men attacked the city of Lyrnessus, taking as a prize two of their most beautiful women, Cryeis and Briseis.

For nine years the Greeks fought the impenetrable walls of Troy, guarded zealously by fine men of battle, including Hector, who led King Priam's other forty-nine sons in war. Paris joined their ranks, although the fury at this selfish man was ill-concealed by many.

Antenor and Aeneas were men of wisdom and justice, and they too fought for Troy, although peace was their ultimate goal. The walls of the city had been built by Apollo and Poseidon themselves, and could not be damaged or scaled, despite the best efforts of Agamemnon's army. So the men of Greece attacked the allies of Troy instead, burning and looting their cities, and ravishing their women. It was at one such rape that a quarrel occurred which would change forever the course of the battle, drawing it to a fiery close that had been nearly a decade in coming.

Achilles and his men had attacked the city of Lyrnessus, taking as their prize two beautiful young women, Cryseis, who was chosen by Agamemnon, and Briseis, who became Achilles's. When it was discovered that the maiden Cryseis was a priestess of Apollo, a plague struck the camp, and Agamemnon was forced to return her to the temple. This he did, but upon his return, he stealthily lured Briseis from the camp of Achilles, and took her as his own. Achilles was so enraged and disgusted by this act that he threw down his armour and swore that he would no longer fight for such men, no better than pigs as they were.

Achilles was a fighter beyond compare and his absence pressed upon the Trojans an unexpected advantage. But the years of war had taken their toll, and the warriors on both sides had grown tired of the hostility. A peaceful end was sought, and Hector appeared, bravely suggesting that Menelaus and Paris fight a dual in order to decide the fate of Helen. This course was considered fair, and the two men engaged in a battle. Swords clashed, and many maidens fainted at the sight of two such glorious men tempting death so readily, so easily. They were well matched, but Menelaus had the power of a grudge that had festered for many years, and with this advantage, he pinned Paris to the walls of his city, determined to take his self-seeking life.

But Aphrodite could stand the battle no longer, and Paris's life was a sacrifice she would not allow. With flowing locks and gowns, she descended on the fighters, her beauty lighting their faces, filling their hearts with surprise and calm. And then she struck, hiding her beloved behind a cloud and pulling him to safety behind the city walls. Menelaus looked on in amazement, so close had he come after all these years to reclaiming his bride, and here the gods took them as their playthings, changing the course of fate, of mortal lives, on a whim. He cried out in rage, a call that was heard by the rest of the gods, and which opened up a wound that would not be healed until the end of the war was in sight.

Thetis screamed for justice for her son Achilles, and Apollo fell in with the defenders, making them strong. Zeus had taken the side of the invaders, who in their eager fury wounded both Ares and Aphrodite, spilling their immortal blood. The Greeks continued to fight, and in a night raid managed to take the life of Rhesus, capturing the white horses which he was taking to the Trojans under the cover of darkness. Apollo swooped down to encourage the Trojan forces, and they repaid this travesty by burning some of the Greek ships, which had been moored in the harbour. And as the fleet burned and threatened the lives of the Greek army, Patroclus, the great friend of Achilles, appeared in his friend's armour, and frightened the Trojans into retreat.

Forgetting himself, and confident in the armour of Greece's greatest warrior, Patroclus leapt to the top of the Trojan walls, sending their army into panic that was calmed only by Apollo. Once more this great god took the side of the Trojans, and knowing that this brave warrior was none other than Patroclus, he winded him, knocking from his body the sword and shield which protected him. Patroclus called out

Opposite: Polyxena, the daughter of King Priam and his Queen Hecabe, was sacrificed at the tomb of Achilles, to appease his ghost.

in anguish, begging for mercy, his bravado shorn from him along with the armour, but Hector stepped in and killed Patroclus with one single blow.

The roar of the Greeks wakened the slumbering Achilles, who had thrust from his mind all thought of the battle. Word of the death of his dear friend soon reached him, and he sprang into action, crying out for revenge which struck terror in the hearts of all who heard him. He trembled with rage, his blood coursing through his veins as he flexed his mighty muscles. New armour was summoned and he dressed quickly, making his way to Troy without delay.

And again the gods chose to intervene. As the terrified Trojans retreated into their city, the river god of the Scamander produced a wall of water that held back the murderous aggressor. This act was met by Hephaestus, who immediately stepped in to dry the waters with a flaming torch. And with a lust for revenge more invincible than the brave Achilles himself, he fought on, searching out the unfortunate Hector and slaying all who crossed his path. Sweat gleamed on his brow, which was furrowed with determination. Achilles presented a picture of such manly beauty that many of his opponents were stopped in their tracks, transfixed by this vision of glorious power. And when Hector saw Achilles, he too stopped dead, and bowed down, determined to fight him hand to hand until he saw that fiery gleam in Achilles' eye and knew that this marauder and his army meant his own certain death. He turned on his heels, and tried to run, but Achilles was stronger, more powerful. Three times they ran round the walls of the city, Hector becoming weaker, more frightened as they ran. And then Achilles caught him, and pinning him like a rabbit to the wall with his sword, howled a mighty cry then thrust his sword through Hector and killed him at once.

The Trojans moaned and wailed for their lost leader, stopping the battle briefly to mourn before swearing vengeance and carrying on more furiously than before. Achilles was unstoppable. When Penthesileia brought her Amazon women to help the Trojans, Achilles killed her mercilessly. And then Thersites, the nasty politician was struck down by Achilles' powerful fist. The invincible Achilles fought on and on, never tiring, never losing his composure, his cunning. Then Memnon arrived with a troop of Ethiopians, putting the favour of the gods once more with the Trojans, who allowed their forces to be increased so heavily. But Achilles, enraged and irreverent, called upon Zeus to judge between himself and Memnon, to reverse the damage done by these visiting troops.

Opposite: And the great city of Troy was dead, her fires glowing for all to see, a warning to lovers and men of war which would live in their memories for the rest of time.

Memnon was out of favour with the king of gods, and Achilles was presented with a sword with which to slay the Ethiopian. And when he died, his followers turned immediately to birds, and followed him to his rocky tomb on the neck of the island.

Achilles continued on, more boastful than ever, never losing a battle, never missing a stroke with his mighty sword. And then the gods lost patience, and irritated by his show of pride, they stepped in once again. Apollo had not yet repaid Achilles for the death of Tenes. Now was his chance. Guiding the hand of Paris, an arrow was directed to the heel of Achilles, the only part on his body which was not invincible. He died immediately.

For a time, the Greeks were weakened by the death of their hero, their determination dwindling, their lust for battle dead. But as they mourned their forsaken leader, a new resolve grew in their hearts, and after a solemn funeral, at which Achilles was awarded the highest honours of any warrior, they regrouped to plan their revenge. If their heart had been cut from them, their mind still functioned. They were supremely competent strategists, extremely confident aggressors. Menelaus appeared to remind them once again of the reason for their battle, and thus inspired they set about deciding whom should take on the arms of Achilles. Agamemnon chose Odysseus, for his intelligence and courage, but Ajax the Greater was steeped in jealousy, knowing his strength was greater than that of Odysseus, beyond all doubt. He swore to avenge himself against Odysseus, but Athene, always a friend to Odysseus, persuaded him in another direction, and thinking he was murdering Odysseus and his troops, he slaughtered instead a flock of sheep. Convinced of his own madness, Ajax took his own life, another untimely and worrying loss to the Greeks.

The war had gone on too long. Zeus had planned it from beginning to end, but now he stopped to appraise, to ensure that the balance was correct. Troy must fall, he decreed, but it could not be achieved without the bow and arrows from the quiver of Heracles, and without the presence of Achilles' son, far away in Scyros. The Greeks moved swiftly. And as they set about summoning Neoptolemus, the son of Achilles, from his home, they

Opposite: And the great horse was dragged into the city, and into the temple of Athene, where it was wreathed with ribbons and festooned with garlands of herbs.

were warned of one final condition, without which the war could not be won. The Palladium must be removed from the city, for she guarded the gates and protected her from all invaders. Odysseus began to plan.

Philoctetes was rescued from his terrible ordeal on Lemnos, his wounds long since cleared. He had trained his mind and his muscles

while he waited impatiently to be saved, and he was anxious to fight, to use the bow of the great Heracles in battle. He lifted it now, spitting on his palms as he did so, and feeding a poisoned arrow into the string of the bow. With a shriek that released the years of tortuous loneliness and pain, he sent the arrow straight to its mark at the neck of the handsome Paris, who was felled at once. And so Neoptolemus was dressed in his father's armour, a shaking, frightened youth with no knowledge of war, no interest in fighting, but he took courage from the dress of his father, and he rose to the challenge, calmly leading his restored army towards the gates of Troy.

Odysseus was busy elsewhere. Dressed as a miserly beggar, with the help of Athene and Diomedes, he talked himself through the gates of the great city, where he fell upon the sleeping guards of the Palladium with such speed and grace that not one person in the entire city knew of his treachery. And on his stomach, he crawled from the city, dragging the Palladium with him, through a vermin-ridden drain where he struggled through sewage and mud to reach his army on the other side, the Palladium drawn triumphantly behind him.

Troy was on the verge of defeat. The Palladium no longer cast its splendid power over the city, and without that advantage, and with the minds of such cunning men as Odysseus to contend, there was no hope. But still she stood firm against the invaders, until Odysseus, with the help of Athene once again, came up with a final plan.

The craftsman Epeius was commissioned to build an enormous wooden horse, the inside of which was hollowed to hold fifty warriors. Agamemnon chose his greatest men to ride in its belly, and then gathering up the remainder of his fleet, he made as if to sail away, leaving the bay at Troy, but travelling only round the bend of the land, where he waited with anticipation and many prayers. Sinon was left behind on land, and as expected, he was taken prisoner by the Trojans, who wondered at their sudden luck. Sinon feigned fury at his colleagues who had left him behind, and taking the side of the Trojans, he wormed his way into their affections, into their grace, so that when he suggested they take into their walls the wooden horse, they did so, marvelling at its inscription:

A thank-offering to Athene for our safe return home.

Again, it was Cassandra who spoke out against the enemy's soldier, proclaiming that the horse brought nothing but death and

Opposite: King Priam was murdered as he crossed his own courtyard – and by moonlight, when the city glowed with a numbing slumber, the massacre of the Trojans began.

final disaster for the city. The prophet Laocoon agreed with her, but as he made his way to the palace to warn the king, he was strangled by two serpents who leapt from the sea, and disappeared once they had finished their deadly task. And the great horse was dragged into the city, into the temple of Athene, where it was wreathed with ribbons and festooned with garlands of herbs.

The Trojans feasted that night, revelling and celebrating the end of a war that had taken quite small toll, despite its very long duration. Inside the wooden horse, the men of Greece laid quietly, waiting for darkness to fall, for their opportunity to strike. Helen alone remained suspicious, knowing that the Greeks were too clever, too ambitious to give in before the bitter end, and she held a grudging admiration for their daring, whatever it may be. She suspected the horse, and late in the evening, she slipped into the darkened temple and called out in the voices of the wives of the men inside, tempting them to come out and be reunited. Only the shrewd Odysseus guessed her trick, and holding his hand over the mouth of each hero who was addressed in false voice, he kept them quiet and soon Helen went away.

The Trojan men were drunk and sleepy when the men slid from the horse on ropes they had prepared earlier. And it was by moonlight, when the city was glowing with a numbing slumber, that the massacre of the Trojans began. King Priam was murdered as he crossed his courtyard, Menelaus went straight to the chambers of his errant wife, who bowed her head and spoke words of such regret, such honest remorse, that the determination in Menelaus was stilled, and he reached out to her and held her again in his arms, transfixed by her beauty, a slave to her love once more.

All was forgiven, and he carried Helen to his ship where she was welcomed into the arms of the Greeks, her fair face disarming them.

The plundering of Troy continued. Women were taken as prizes by the men of Greece who had for so long been starved of female companionship. Cassandra was taken by Agamemnon, and Neoptolemus who had grown in his weeks with the army to become a noble youth, took Hector's widow Andromache. Polyxena was sacrificed at the tomb of Achilles, to appease his ghost. Aeneas was wounded fatally, but the gods swooped to him and healed him. Apollo urged him to challenge the marauders, but Poseidon spoke softly to him, prophesying a day when he would rule Troy. And so Aeneas left the burning city, losing his wife in the escape, his subsequent travels becoming the subject of Roman legends, and Vergil's flawless Aeneid.

Queen Hecabe sat in her tower window watching the massacre, the deaths of her family, her colleagues, her servants and their children. And when Odysseus took her as his own, her howls of pure despair reached to the heavens and she was transformed magically into a dog, whose barks could be heard on the shores of Troy for all eternity.

Troy was broken, its streets steeped in the blood of generations of warriors, its walls finally scaled and broken, pouring out the good will and good luck that had been held in her embrace since the very beginning. She was set alight by zealous Greeks, a blazing beacon to all who knew her, her heart beating no longer.

So it was that Helen returned to Sparta with Menelaus, where they were reunited. Other great heroes went their separate ways, many returning to glory, carrying the spoils of their victory in treasure-laden ships. Still others met with disaster on their voyage home, but those are other stories, legends which were spawned by the war of Troy. And the great city of Troy was dead, her fires glowing for all to see, a warning to lovers and to the men of war which would live in their memories for the rest of time.

※　※　※

THE WANDERING OF ODYSSEUS
THE JOURNEY

 lushed with the glory of his victory at Troy, the brave and clever Odysseus gathered together the men of Ithaca into twelve ships, and headed across the perilous seas to their homeland. Odysseus was the grandson of the Autolycus, a thief of great artfulness and notoriety. That same cunning lay deep within the breast of Odysseus and it would, said the Oracle before Odysseus set off for Troy, bring about his solitary survival. For Odysseus alone would return from Troy, beaten and infinitely weary, having battled the great gods of the sea and sky and winds, having faced temptations and fears which would bring about the certain death of a lesser man. The journey would take ten years, and its cost would be Odysseus's men and very nearly his soul.

The Cicones

The fate of every chief beside
Who fought at Troy is known:
It is the will of Jove to hide
His untold death alone.

And how he fell can no man tell;
We know not was he slain
In fight on land by hostile hand,
Or plunged beneath the man.

MAGINN'S HOMERIC BALLADS

TEN YEARS HAD PAST since brave Odysseus had last set eyes on his faithful wife Penelope, and their son Telemachus. The victory at Troy had been a sweet one, and sated by the triumph, the lean and weathered warrior made plans to return his men to their homeland. Twelve ships were prepared for the voyage, laden with the spoils of their warfare and leaving the wretched and burning city of Troy a blazing beacon behind them.

Odysseus and his men were filled with rumbustuous excitement at the prospect of seeing home once more; they leapt and frolicked aboard the mighty vessels, unable to leave behind the boisterous energy nurtured in them by ten years' war. The sea lay calm and welcoming. The journey had begun, and the ships groaned with booty.

But greed is a fatal human trait, and not content with the plunder they had foraged at Troy, Odysseus and his men sought new bounty, landing first on the island of the Cicones. A mass of carousing warriors, they swept onshore, taking the city of Ismarus, sending its inhabitants to their deaths, and feasting on the carcasses of their sheep and cattle. Only the priest of Apollo was spared from the carnage.

This priest was a clever man, and he sank to his knees in gratitude, bowing his head in respectful silence as he supplied the marauders with skins of powerful wine. While the men feasted and celebrated the newest of their victories, Odysseus grew increasingly uneasy. Although he shared the piratical spirit of his men, he had an ingrown prudence which argued against the excesses of their plundering. He implored his men to return to their ships, doubting now the wisdom of their attack. Soon enough his worries were confirmed.

As the men of Ithaca lay spent and drunk on wine and rich foods,

Opposite: Twelve ships were prepared for the voyage, laden with the spoils of their warfare and leaving the wretched city of Troy a burning beacon behind them

the Cicones appeared on the hilltops, eager for revenge and accompanied by troops they had rallied from the islands around their country. Odysseus tried to rouse his men, but his efforts were futile. The Cicones attacked, driving the disoriented travellers back to their ship, mercilessly slaying those who lagged behind. The carnage took tremendous toll on the crews of each ship, and lamed by defeat they limped out of the harbour and back to sea. Back aboard ship, the surviving men worked quietly, bewildered by the proof of their humanity, their weakness. Home lay just round the Cape at the point of the Peloponnese. But as anticipation rose within them, so did the savage gales of the north-east winds. Zeus, king of the gods, would wreak his vengeance.

The Lotus-Eaters

Branches they bore of that enchanted stem,
Laden with flower and fruit, whereof they gave
To each, but whoso did receive of them,
And taste, to him the gushing of the wave
Far, far away did seem to mourn and rave
On alien shores; and if his fellow spake,
His voice was thin, as voices from the grave;
And deep-asleep he seem'd, yet all awake,
And music in his ears his beating heart did make.

ALFRED, LORD TENNYSON

THE POWERFUL WINDS wrenched and buffeted the wretched ships, carrying them and their dispirited crew far from the point of the Cape, ever further from the welcoming shores of Ithaca. The sails were torn, and desperation clung to the men as they struggled against the most powerful of enemies – the sea and the winds themselves. And then, on the tenth day, there was peace. Just beyond the curve of the gentle waves lay land, a southern island from which a pervading and sweet perfume rose languorously into the air.

Ever watchful, Odysseus dared send ashore only three men from his depleted crew, and the men prepared the boat, their hearts beating. As their oars cut softly through the waves, an eerie and disquieting lassitude overwhelmed the men. Their trembling hands were warmed and stilled, their hearts were calmed in their breasts. And there, in front of them, appeared a remarkable being, whose serenity and stillness relaxed the anxious sailors, With a smile the creature beckoned them forth, holding out to them as he signalled, a large and purple flower.

Opposite: Odysseus's men lolled with a group of beautiful beings. There was no anger or fear among them. They smiled a beatific welcome and signalled that he was to join them.

The perfume of the flower snaked around the men, entrancing them and drawing them forth.

'The lotus flower,' the creature whispered softly. 'Sip its nectar. It is our food and drink here on the island of the lotus-eaters. It brings peace.' With that the lotus-eater raised the flower to the mouths of the men, who one by one drank deeply from its cup. Expressions of pure joy crossed their faces and their minds and memories were cleared of all but the rich and overwhelming pleasures of the nectar.

'It is the food of forgetfulness,' smiled the lotus-eater. 'Come, join us in the land of indolence. We have no worries here.'

Odysseus stood on the prow of his ship, a shadow of concern crossing his noble brow. 'Remain here,' he ordered his men, his voice unusually curt. His senses were buzzing with anticipation. He could feel an uneasy melancholy touching at the corners of his mind, and he angrily shrugged it away. All was not well on the island. He could sense no violence here, but danger lurked in a different cloak. He made his way to shore.

There was no sign of his sailors, and he strode purposefully in the direction he'd seen them take. He fought the growing ease which threatened to fill his mind, the strength of his character, his cunning forcefully keeping the invading sensations at bay. His men lolled by the fire of a group of beautiful beings. There was no anger or fear among them. They smiled a beatific welcome and signalled that he was to join them. A lotus flower was held up for him to drink, and as he softened, a bell of fear rang in his brain. He curled back his lips and with renewed resolve, thrust the flower away. He drew from his pocket a length of rope, and hastily tied it to the scabbards of his men. He ignored their weak protests, and with his sword in their bags, forced them back to shore, and to the ship.

Their eyes were vague, their smiles bloodless. Odysseus and his men were as strangers to them, but they went aboard ship where they were lashed to the masts until the ship could sail on. The enchantment raised the heads of every man aboard Odysseus's ships. He roared at them to keep their heads down, to pierce their longing with good clean thoughts.

'Think of home, men,' he shouted. 'Forget it not, for it is what fires us onwards.'

And so they were to escape the fruit of the lotus-eaters, and the life of ease that threatened to overcome them. Odysseus and his men, weakened but still alive, sailed on.

The Cyclopes

So till the sun fell we did drink and eat,
And all night long beside the billows lay,
Till blush'd the hills 'neath morning's rosy feet;
Then did I bid my friends, with break of day,
Loosen the hawsers, and each bark array;
Who take the benches, and the whitening main
Cleave with the sounding oars, and sail away.
So from the isle we part, not void of pain,
Right glad of our own lives, but grieving for the slain.

WORSLEY

ODYSSEUS AND HIS MEN sailed until they were forced to stop for food and fresh water. A small island appeared in the distance, and as they drew nigh, they saw that it was inhabited only by goats, who fed on the succulent, sweet grass which grew plentifully across the terrain. Fresh water cascaded from moss-carpeted rocks, and tumbled through the leafy country. The men's lips grew wet in anticipation of its cold purity.

As they clambered aboard shore, the fresh air filling their lungs, the men felt whole once more, and when they discovered, in their travels, an inviting cave filled with goats' milk and cheese, they settled down to feast. Their bellies groaning, and faces pink with pleasure, Odysseus and his men settled back to sleep on the smooth face of the cave, warmed by the hot spring that pooled in its centre, and sated by their sumptuous meal.

They were woken abruptly by heavy footfall, which shook the ground with each step. Eyeing one another warily, the tired men stayed silent, barely alert, but overwhelmingly fearful. Into the cave burst a flock of snow-white sheep and behind them the frightful giant Polyphemus, a Cyclops with one eye in the centre of his face. Polyphemus was the son of Poseidon, and he lived on the island with his fellow Cyclopes, existing peacefully in seclusion. He had not seen man for many years, and his single eyebrow raised in anticipation when he came upon his visitors.

Odysseus took charge.

'Sire, in the name of Zeus, I beg your hospitality for the night. I've weary men who ...'

His words were cut off. The Cyclops laughed with outrage and reaching over, plucked up several of Odysseus's men and ate them whole. The others cowered in fear, but Odysseus stood firm, his stance betraying none of the fear that surged through his noble blood.

'I ask you again,' he began. But Polyphemus merely grunted and turned to roll a boulder across the opening to the cave. He settled down to sleep, his snores lifting the men from the stone floor of the cave, and forbidding them sleep. They huddled round Odysseus, who pondered their plight.

When he woke, Polyphemus ate two more men, and with his sheep, left the cave, carefully closing the door on the anxious men. They moved around their prison with agitation, wretched with fear. It was many hours before the Cyclops returned, but the men could not sleep. They waited for the sound of footsteps, they sickened at the thought of their inescapable death.

But the brave Odysseus feared not. His cunning led him through the maze of their predicament, and carefully and calmly he formed a plan. He was waiting when Polyphemus returned, and sidled up to the weary Cyclops with his goatskin of wine.

'Have a drink, ease your fatigue,' he said quietly, and with surprise the giant accepted. Unused to wine, he fell quickly into confusion, and laid himself unsteadily on the floor of the cave.

'Who are you, generous benefactor,' he slurred, clutching at the goatskin.

'My name is No one,' said Odysseus, a satisfied smile fleeting across his face.

'No one ...' the giant repeated the name and slipped into a deep slumber, his snores jolting the men once more.

Odysseus leapt into action. Reaching for a heavy bough of olive-wood, he plunged in into the fire and moulded its end to a barbed point. He lifted it from the fire, and with every ounce of strength and versatility left in his depleted body, he thrust it into Polyphemus' single eye, and stepped back, out of harm's way.

The Cyclops' roar propelled him through the air, momentarily deafening him. The men shuddered in the corner, shrieking with terror as the giant fumbled wildly for his torturers, grunting and shrieking with the intense pain. Soon his friends came running, and when they enquired the nature of his troubles, he could only cry, 'No one has blinded me' at which they returned, perplexed to their homes.

The morning came, cool and inviting, and hearing his sheep scrabbling at the door to get out to pasture, Polyphemus rose, and feeling

Opposite: The torment of the giant rose in a deluge of sound and fury, echoing across the island and wakening his friends. Polyphemus roared a prayer to his father Poseidon.

along the walls, he found his boulder, and moved it. A smug look crossed his tortured features, and he stood outside the cave, his hands moving across the sheep as they left.

'You cannot leave this cave,' he taunted. 'You cannot escape me now.' He giggled with mirth at his cleverness, but his smile faded to confusion and then anger when he realized that the sheep had exited, and the cave was now empty. The men were gone.

Odysseus and his men laughed out loud as they unstrapped themselves from the bellies of the sheep, and racing towards their ships, Odysseus called out, 'Cyclops. It was not No one who blinded you. It was Odysseus of Ithaca,' and with that he lifted their mooring and set out for sea.

The torment of the giant rose in a deluge of sound and fury, echoing across the island and wakening his friends. Tearing off slabs of the mountainside, Polyphemus hurled them towards the escaping voice, which continued to taunt him. He roared a prayer to his father Poseidon, begging for vengeance, and struggled across the grass towards the sea.

But Odysseus had left, his ship surging across the sea to join with the rest of the fleet. Odysseus had escaped once more, and the sea opened up to him and his men, and they continued homewards, unaware that Poseidon had heard the cries of his son, and had answered them. Vengeance would be his.

The Island of Aeolus

ODYSSEUS AND THE REST of his fleet were carried out to sea by the swell of water which spread from the rocks which Polyphemus had plunged into the waters. His cries echoed across the waters, growing louder as he realized the full measure of Odysseus's treachery, for as he and his men left they had robbed him of most of his flock, which they now cooked on spits over roaring fires in the galley.

They sailed to the Island of Aeolus, the guardian of winds, who lived with his six sons and six daughters in great comfort. Here, Odysseus and his men were entertained and feted, fed with sumptuous buffets which boasted unusual delicacies, their thirst slaked by fine wines and exotic nectars. They remained there for thirty days, convincing Aeolus that the gods must detest these men for unfounded reasons., for they were perfect guests, and Odysseus was a fair man, and an eloquent spokesman and orator.

But at last Odysseus grew restless, eager once more to set sail for Ithaca. The generosity of Aeolus had calmed his men, and well-nourished they were ready to do battle with the elements which were bound to hamper their return. But Aeolus had a gift for Odysseus, which he presented as the men prepared to leave the island. With great solemnity he passed to the warrior a bag, carefully bound with golden lace, and knotted many times over. In it were secured all the winds, except the gentle winds of the west, which would blow them to Ithaca. It was a sacred gift, and a token of Aeolus's regard for his visitor.

The men set off at last, their bellies filled, their minds alert, all maladies relieved. They sailed, blown by the west wind, for nine days, until the bright shores of Ithaca shone, a brilliant beacon in the distance. And so it was that Odysseus, greatly fatigued by the journey, and by the excitement of reaching his native shores once more, allowed himself to rest, to fall into a deep slumber that would prepare him for the festivities about to greet him.

But several of the men who sailed under his command begrudged their gracious leader, and envious of his favour with Aeolus, decided to take for themselves some of the gift presented to Odysseus. It must contain treasure, they thought, so large and unwieldy a parcel it was, and the men encouraged one another, fantasizing about what that bag might contain.

And so it was that the men tiptoed to Odysseus's chambers, and eased the bag from his side, careful not to disturb his slumber. And it was with greedy smiles, and anxious, fumbling hands that the bag was opened and the fierce winds released. They swirled around them, tossing and plunging the ships into waves higher than the mountains of the gods. In no time they were returned to the Island of Aeolus, helpless and frightened by nature's angry howls.

Odysseus was roughly awakened, and pushed forward to greet the displeased Aeolus. Aeolus cursed himself for humouring such foolish men, and understood at last the antipathy felt towards them by the great powers of Greece.

'Be gone, ill-starred wretch,' he snarled, and turned away from the unhappy seamen, towards the confines of his palace.

And so there was nothing for it but to return to the merciless seas, where the winds played havoc in their renewed freedom, where Poseidon waited for his chance to strike.

The Laestrygonians

THE SHIPS OF ODYSSEUS and his men were buffeted for many days before the winds exhausted their breath. And so they abandoned the ill-fated travellers, and left them in a dreadful calm. The ships sat still, mired in the stagnant waters, sunburnt and parched by the fiery sun. For a week they struggled with the heavy oars, seeming to move no further across the waveless sea. And then, on the eighth day, their ships limped into the rocky harbour of the Laestrygonians, where they moored themselves in an untidy row and made their way to shore. Odysseus was more cautious. Their travels had made him wiser than ever, and he tied his boat beyond the others, to a rocky outcrop in the open water.. He signalled the men aboard to hold back, and climbed up the mast to get a better view.

Three of his men had rowed ashore, and Odysseus watched them as they spoke to two lovely young maidens, drawing water from a clear spring. The men stopped to take a drink before pressing on in the direction pointed out to them by the maidens. They looked calm and assured. Odysseus felt no such conviction, and he remained where he was, chewing his lower lip with concern. His men could see the others, and pestered Odysseus to allow them ashore, to drink of the cool fresh water, but he bade them to be silent and returned to his look-out.

The three men were easily visible from his post and Odysseus could see them reaching the walls of a magnificent castle, gilded and festooned with jewels. They hesitated at the gates. And it was then that the Laestrygonians attacked. Great, heaving giants plummeted through the gates on to the hapless men, racing towards shore and wailing a terrible cry, a battle song that tweaked at Odysseus's memory. These were the the evil cannibals who brought overwhelming fear to the heart of every traveller. Their shores were the most dangerous in Greece, their fearsome appetite for violence and unwitting seamen legendary.

They stampeded to shore, flocking in crowds to crush the ships under a deluge of rocks and spears. The sailors were skewered like lambs, and plucked from the waters, swallowed whole or sectioned and dipped into a bath of melted sheep's fat which lay bubbling in a cauldron beside the shores. The Laestrygonians had received word of Odysseus's ships and were prepared for the feast. They splashed and howled, laughing and eating until every one of Odysseus's comrade's ships was destroyed, emptied of its human cargo which presented such a cruel breakfast.

Opposite: The men were easily visible from his post and Odysseus could see them reaching the walls of a magnificent castle.

Odysseus had long since cut the ropes which anchored him to the rocks, and he and his crew raced for the deep sea, rowing faster than any mortal before them. Flushed with fear, their hearts pounding, they rowed for two days, one single crew saved from the tortures of the Laestrygonians by the wit of their captain. They rowed until they reached the shores of another island, where they collapsed, unable to lift their weary heads, caring not if in their refuge they courted danger.

Circe and the Island of Aeaea

On his bloomy face
Youth smil'd celestial, with each opening grace.
He seiz'd my hand and gracious thus began:
'Ah! whither roam'st thou, much enduring man?
O blind to fate! What led thy steps to rove
The horrid mazes of this magic grove?
Each friend you seek in yon inclosure lies,
All lost their form, and habitants of sties.
Think'st thou by wit to model their escape?
Sooner shalt thou, a stranger to thy shape,
Fall prone their equal: first they danger know:
Then take the antidote the gods bestow ...

ALEXANDER POPE

FOR NEARLY TWO DAYS the men slept on the shores of the unknown island, drinking in the peacefulness which covered them like a blanket, coming to terms with the loss of their comrades in their dreams. They woke freshened, but wary, eager to explore the land, but made prudent by their misadventures. In the distance, smoke curled lethargically into the windless sky. The island was inhabited, but by whom?

Odysseus divided the group into two camps, one taken by himself, the other led by his lieutenant, the courageous and loyal warrior Eurylochus. They drew lots from a helmet, and so it was decreed that Eurylochus would lead his party into the forest, towards the signs of life. His men gathered themselves up, and brushed off their clothes, trembling with anticipation and fear. They moved off.

The path wound its way through the tree-clad island, drawing the men into the bosom of the hills. There, at its centre, was a roughly

Opposite: Their knocks were greeted by the figure of a beautiful woman, her hair tumbling to her heels, eyes two green jewels in an ivory facade.

hewn cottage, chimney smoking, and no sign of danger. Its fine stone walls were guarded by wolves and lions, but they leapt playfully towards the explorers, licking them and wagging their tails. Confused but comforted by the welcome, the men drew forward, and soon were enticed by the exquisite melody which drifted from the cottage. A woman's voice rang out, pure and sweet, calming their hearts, and drying the sweat on their brows. They moved forward confidently, only Eurylochus hanging back in caution.

They were greeted by the figure of a beautiful woman, whose hair tumbled to her heels, whose eyes were two green jewels in an ivory facade. Her smile was benevolent, welcoming, her arms outstretched. The men stumbled over one another to greet her, and were led into the cavernous depths of the cottage, where tables groaned with luxurious morsels of food – candied fruits, roasted spiced meats, plump vegetables and glazed breads, tumbling from platters of silver and gold. Wines and juices glistened in frosted glasses, and a barrel of fine brandy dripped into platinum goblets. It was a feast beyond compare, and the aroma enveloped the men, drawing them forward. They ate and drank while Eurylochus waited uncomfortably, outside the gates. And after many hours, when the men had taken their fill, they sat back with smiles of contentment, of satisfied gluttony, and raised their eyes in gratitude to their hostess.

'Who are you, fine woman?' slurred one of the crewman, made bold by the spirits.

'I am Circe,' she whispered back. And with a broad sweep of her hand, and a cry of laughter which startled her guests, drawing them from their stupor, she shouted, ' And you are but swine, like all men.'

Circe was a great and beautiful enchantress, living alone on this magical island where all visitors were pampered and fed with a charmed repast until Circe grew bored with them. And then, stroking their stupid heads, Circe would make them beasts. Now, she raised her mighty hands and laid them down upon the heads of Eurylochus's men and turned them to swine, corralling them snuffling and grunting through the door. Eurylochus peered round a tree in dismay. Ten men had entered, and now ten pigs left. The enchantress followed them, penning them in sties and stopping to speak gently to the other beasts, who had once been men. Happily she returned to her cottage and took up her loom once more.

Opposite: I am Circe,' she whispered back. And with a broad sweep of her hand, and a cry of laughter, she shouted, 'And you are but swine ...'

Eurylochus sprinted through the forest, breathless with fear and disbelief as he rejoined Odysseus and the crew. Odysseus drew himself up, and a determined look transformed his distinguished

features. He reached for his sword, and thrusting a dagger in his belt he set off to rescue his men, turning his head heavenwards and praying for assistance from the very gods who had spurned him. Odysseus had suffered the insults of war, and the tortures of their perilous journey. He would fight for his men, for his depleted crew. No woman, enchantress or not, would outwit him, would take from him his few remaining men.

As he struggled through the forest, a youth stumbled across his path.

'Here,' he whispered. 'Take this.' And he thrust into the hands of Odysseus a divine herb known as Moly, a plant with black roots and a snow white flower so beautiful that only those with celestial hands had the strength to pluck it. Moly was an antidote against the spells of Circe, and with this in his possession, Odysseus would be safe. The boy, who was really the god Hermes, sent by the goddess Athene, warned Odysseus of Circe's magical powers, and offered him a plan.

And so it was that Odysseus reached the cottage of Circe, and entered its welcoming gates. There the same feast greeted him, and he partook of the food until he lay sleepy and sated. Circe could hardly disguise her glee at the ease with which she had trapped this new traveller, and as she waved her wand to change him into a pig, Odysseus rose and spoke.

'Your magic has no power over me,' he said, and he thrust her to the ground at the point of his sword.

She trembled with fear, and with longing.

'You,' she breathed, 'you must be the brave Odysseus, come from far to be my loving friend.' And she threw down her wand and took the soldier into her warm embrace. They lay together for a night of love, and in the morning, spent yet invigorated by their carnal feast they rose to set free Odysseus's men.

And there, on the enchanted island of Circe, Odysseus and his men spent days which stretched into golden weeks and then years, fed from the platters laden with food, their glasses poured over with drink, resting and growing fat, until they had forgotten the tortures of their journey. Odysseus was charmed by the lovely Circe, and all thoughts of Penelope and Telemachus were chased from his mind. His body was numbed by the pleasures inflicted upon it.

Opposite: The enchantress followed them, penning them in sties and stopping to speak to the other beasts who had once been men.

But the great Odysseus was a supreme leader, and even pure indulgence could not blunt his keen mind forever. As his senses gradually cleared, as Circe's powers over his body, over his soul began

to wane, he felt the first rush of homesickness, of longing for Ithaca and his family. And in his heart he began to feel the weight of his responsibilities, the burden of his obligations to his country, to his men and to the gods.

With that, he made secret plans for their escape, and as the enchantment began also to wear at the sanity of his men, as they grew tired of the hedonism which filled their every waking hour, they became party to his strategy. With that, he went in search of Circe.

The House of Hades

ODYSSEUS FOUND THE ENCHANTRESS Circe in a calm and equable mood. She loved Odysseus, who had warmed her heart and her bed, but she had known since first setting eyes on the great warrior that he could never be completely hers. This day had been long in coming, but now that it was upon her, she gave him her blessing.

There were, however, tasks to be undertaken before Odysseus could be freed. He and his men could not voyage to Ithaca until they had met with the ghost of the blind prophet Tiresias, wiser than any dead or alive. They must travel to him at Hades, bringing gifts to sacrifice to the powers of the Underworld. Whitened by fear the men agreed to journey with Odysseus, to learn their fate and to receive instructions for their return to Ithaca.

All his men, spare one, prepared themselves for the voyage, but Elpenor, the youngest of the crew, lay sleeping on the roof of the cottage, where he'd stumbled in a drunken stupor the previous night. He woke to see the ship and his comrades setting sail from the island of Circe, and forgetting himself, he tumbled to the ground where he met an instant and silent death.

The men pressed on, unaware that one of their lot was missing. They sailed through a fair wind, raised by Circe, and as darkness drew itself around them, they entered the deep waters of Oceanus, where the Cimmerians lived in eternal night. There the rivers Phlegethon, Cocytus and Styx converged beneath a great rock, and Odysseus and his men drew aground. Following Circe's instructions, they dug a deep well in the earth beside the rock, then they cut the throats of a ram and a ewe, allowing their virgin blood to fill the trough.

The ghosts of the departed began to gather round the blood, some in battle-stained garb, others lost and confused; they struggled up to the pit and fought for a drink. Odysseus drew his sword to hold back the swelling crowd, startled as Elpenor, pale and blood-spattered, greeted his former master. He pressed forward, moaning and reaching greedily for the mortals.

'I have no grave,' he uttered. 'I cannot rest.' He clung to Odysseus whose cold stare belied the anxiety that pressed down on his heart. He was too close to the wretched creatures of the Underworld, near enough to be dragged down with them. He shook Elpenor loose.

'I will build you a grave,' he said gruffly. 'A fine grave with a tomb. There your ashes will lay and you shall have peace.'

Elpenor pulled back at once, a bemused expression crossing his pale face. He slid away, as reaching arms grappled into the space he left. Faces blended together in a grotesque dance of the macabre, writhing bodies struggling to catch a glimpse of mortals, of the other side. Familiar features appeared and then disappeared, as Odysseus fought to keep control of his senses.

'Odysseus,' the voice was soft, crooning. How often he'd heard it, sheltered in the tender arms of its bearer, rocked, adored. *Mother.*

Anticleia had been alive when he'd sailed for Troy and until this moment he knew not of her death. He longed to reach out for her, to take her pale and withered body against his own, to provide her with the comfort she had so tenderly invested in him.

But his duties prodded at his conscience, and he pricked his sword at her, edging her away from him, searching the tumultuous mass for Tiresias. At last he appeared from the shadowy depths, stopping to drink deeply from the bloody sacrifice. He leaned against his golden staff, and spoke slowly, in a language mellowed with age.

'Odysseus,' Tiresias said. 'Thy homecoming will not be easy. Poseidon bears spite against thee for blinding his Cyclops son Polyphemus. Yet you have guardians, and all may go well still, if, when you reach the hallowed shores of Trinacrian, ye harm not the herds of the Sun that pasture there. Control thy men, Odysseus. Allow not the greed that has tainted their hearts, that has led you astray, to shadow your journey.'

He paused, drinking again from the trenches and shrugging aside the groping arms of his comrades. He spat into the pool of blood.

'If you slay them, Odysseus, you will bring death upon your men, wreckage to your ships, and if you do escape, you will find thy house in trouble, no glory in your homecoming. And in the end, death will come to thee from the sea, from the great Poseidon.' With that, Tiresias leaned heavily on his staff and stumbled away, calling out as he left, 'Mark my words, brave Odysseus. My sight is not hampered by the darkness.'

Odysseus sat down and pondered the blindman's words. Anticleia appeared once again and he beckoned her closer, coaxed her to drink, and with the power invested in her by the blood, she drew a deep breath and spoke. She asked eagerly of his news, and told of her own, how she had died of grief thinking him dead at Troy. But his father, Laertes, she said, was still alive, though weakened by despair and feeble in his old age. Penelope his wife waited for him, loyal despite the attentions of many suitors. And Telemachus had become a man, grown tall and strong like his father.

Odysseus was torn by the sight of his mother, knowing not when he would set eyes on her again. He reached out to touch her, but she shrank from his embrace, a vision only, no substance, no warm blood coursing through her veins. He stood abruptly and was thronged by the clambering dead, as his mother drifted from his sight. He called after her, but she had gone.

Many of his comrades from Troy appeared now, eager to see the fine Odysseus, curious about his presence in Hades without having suffered the indignity of death. There was Agamemnon, and again, Achilles, whose stature was diminished, whose glory had tarnished. Ajax was there, and Tantalus and Sisyphus reached out to him, howling with anguish. And then there was Minos, and Orion, and Hercules, great men once, ghostly spectres now. They circled him and he felt chilled by their emptiness, by their singleness, by their determination to possess him. He turned away and strode from the group, shaking with the effort.

And his men joined him there, as they rowed away from that perilous island, down the Ocean river and back to the open sea. The friendly winds tossed them back to Circe's island, where the enchantress awaited them. Their belongings were ready, and she had resigned herself to the loss of her great love. She pulled Odysseus to one side, stroking him until he stiffened with pleasure, tempted as always to remain with her, enjoyed and enjoying. She whispered in his ear, warning him of the hazards which stood between Aeaea and Ithaca, the perils of his course. And he kissed her deeply and with a great surge of confidence, pushed her aside and went to meet his men.

Together they uncovered the body of poor Elpenor, and burned it

Opposite: The winds tossed them back to Circe's island, and she waited there, resigned to the loss of her great love. She pulled Odysseus to one side, stroking him until he stiffened with pleasure.

with great ceremony, placing his ashes in a grand and sturdy tomb. Their duty done, they looked towards home.

And so it was that Odysseus escaped the fires of Hades, and the clutches of the shrewd Circe, and found himself heading once more towards Ithaca and home, the warnings of Circe and Tiresias echoing in his ears. As chance would have it, the first of the dangers lay just across the shimmering sea.

The Sirens

Come, pride of Achaia, Odysseus, draw night us!
Come, list to our chant, rest the oar from its rowing:
Never yet was there any whose galley fled by us,
But, sweet as the drops from the honeycomb flowing,
Our voices enthralled him, and stayed his ongoing,
And he passed from that rapture more wise than aforetime:
For we know all the toil that in Troyland befell,
When the will of the Gods was wrought out in the war-time:
Yea, all that is done on the earth can we tell.

A.S. WAY

The air was hot and heavy around the vessel; the sunlight glinted on her bow as she cut through the silent sea. The men were restless. The silence held the threat of ill fate and they looked to Odysseus with wary eyes, seeking his wisdom, begging him wordlessly for comfort.

Odysseus stood tall alongside the mast, his noble profile chiselled against the airless horizon. He looked troubled, his head cocked to one side as he heard the first whispers of a beautiful melody.

It stung and tore at his sanity, dredging up a memory, a warning, but lulling him somehow away from his men, from his responsibilities, from the course of his voyage. He struggled against the growing sound, alert to the knowledge that his men had not yet heard its seductive strains but every fibre of his being ached to find its source, to touch its creator.

The Sirens.

Opposite: Odysseus stood tall alongside the mast. He looked troubled as he heard the first whispers of a beautiful melody. The Sirens.

The words leapt to his troubled mind, and with great effort he drew himself from the reverie.

'Lash me to the mast,' he cried suddenly. Something in his voice caused his astonished men to obey.

'But captain, sir ...' one of the younger seamen ventured to express his amazement.

'Now!' Odysseus felt the bewildered hurt of his men. He also heard the growing symphony of the Sirens. He felt himself being drawn back, their melody licking at his mind like the hottest of fires, burning his resolve and his sanity.

'The candles,' he mouthed groggily. 'Melt the candles.' He could barely choke out the words. 'The wax ... in your ears.'

A startled silence was filled by the roaring of Odysseus's first mate: 'Do as he says, men. We have never had cause to question the wisdom of Odysseus. He has the strength and the cunning of ten men. He sees what we cannot see. We must put our faith in him.'

The ears of each man were carefully plugged by the wax of forty candles. As the last man turned his head, a swell of sound filled the air. Odysseus gave himself to it, wrestling with the lashings that restrained his strong frame. The sweet song of death called him, beckoned him from his lofty post.

The Sirens. The birds of death, temptresses of darkness – their sensuous melody played on the chords of his mind, calling him to a blackness which would envelope him forever. They appeared around him, luxuriant hair tumbling about angelic faces. He was trapped in a swarm of soaring wings and resplendent feathers. Women of the birds, with voices to lull even the hardiest warrior to certain death.

The deafened crew of his ship watched in amazement as the elegant creatures swooped among them, their eyes gleaming with secret knowledge, their voices capturing Odysseus in a cloud of passionate yearning.

Befuddled by the play on his senses, Odysseus signalled to his men to begin to row, then he sank back against the mast, spent and sickened by longing. The mighty vessel collected speed, ploughing through the sea that rippled with the thrust of the Sirens and the power of their music.

The sound increased, their music tortuously alluring as the Sirens fought for the spirit of Odysseus. The men battled with their oars, churning the water aside, sensing the danger that had hewn such fear on the face of their leader.

The music of the Sirens took on a rising note of mirth, and then, as the ship surged away from their grips, they laughed aloud.

'You will be ours again,' they sang together, laughing and diving around the fallen man. 'Ours to the end.'

Opposite: The sirens, the birds of death, temptresses of darkness – their sensuous melody played on the chords of his mind, calling him to a blackness which would envelope him forever.

They rose in a cluster of discord and light and disappeared, a painful silence filling the cacophony of sound that was no more. Odysseus rose again. He looked to the east, to the island of the Sirens, and he signalled to his men to clear their ears. He'd had to hear it. Circe had warned him of the Sirens, and although he trusted not the weak natures of his men, he had relished the chance to tempt his own resolve. But it was a bitter triumph, for he'd very nearly been lost to them, tugged so close to the edge of his mind, to madness and the darkness beneath.

A sweet wind caught the main sail and the ship plunged forward. Their small victory raised a smile on the weather-beaten faces of the seamen, and then they turned their faces to waters new.

Scylla and Charybdis

CIRCE HAD WARNED ODYSSEUS of the dangers that would beset him and his crew should they choose to ignore the words of wise Tiresias. The next part of their journey would take them though a narrow strait, peopled by some of the most fearsome monsters in all the lands. Odysseus was to guide the ship through the narrow passage, through fierce and rolling waters, looking neither up nor down, embodying all humility.

But the pride of Odysseus was more deeply rooted than his fear, and ignoring Circe's words, he took a stand on the prow of his ship, heavily armoured and emboldened by the support of his men. Here he stood as they passed the rocks of Charybdis, the hateful daughter of Poseidon, who came to the surface three times each day in order to belch out a powerful whirlpool, drawing into her frothing gut all that came back with it. There was no sign of her now, the waters suspiciously stilled. Ahead lay an island, drenched in warm sunlight, beckoning to the weary sailors. They must just make it through.

Odysseus had kept the details of this fearsome strait from his men. They had been weakened by battle, and by the horrific sights which had met their eyes since leaving Troy. They were so close to Ithaca, he dared not cast their hopes and anticipation into shadow. And so it was that only Odysseus knew of the next monster who was to be thrust upon them in that dangerous channel, only Odysseus who knew that she was capable of tasks more gruesome than any of them had seen in all their travels.

For Scylla was a gluttonous and evil creature that haunted the strait, making her home in a gore-splattered den where she feasted on the remains of luckless sailors. She was, they said, a nymph who had been the object of Glaucus's attentions. Glaucus was a sea-god who had been turned into a merman by a strange herb he had unwittingly swallowed. And as much as he adored Scylla, so he was loved by Circe who, in a jealous rage, had turned Scylla into a terrible sea-monster with six dog's heads around her waist. She lived there in the cliff face in the straits of Messina, and devoured sailors who passed. She moved silently. Odysseus was loath to admit it, but the silent danger she represented placed more fear in his heart than the bravest of enemies.

Odysseus and his men passed further into the quiet strait, their mouths dry with fear. A silence hung over them like a shroud. And then it was broken by a tiny splash, and tinkle of water dripping, and up, with a mighty roar, came Scylla, the mouths on each head gaping open, their lethal jaws sprung for one purpose alone. Smoothly she leaned forward and in a flash of colour, of torn clothing and hellish screams, six of his best men were plucked from their posts aboard ship and drawn into the mouth of her cave. Their cries rent at the heart, at the conscience of Odysseus, and he turned helplessly to his remaining crew who looked at him with genuine fear, distrust and anger. A mutinous fever bubbled at the edges of their loyalty, and Odysseus knew he had lost them. He looked back at the cave where Scylla had silenced his hapless men, and signalled the others to row faster. A repeat of her attack would leave him with too few men to carry on. They rowed towards the shores of the great three-cornered island, Thrinacie, where the herds of the Sun-god Helius grazed peacefully on the hilltops.

The Flock of Helius

SHAKEN BY THE TORTURE of his men, Odysseus proclaimed that they would make no further stops until they reached the shores of Ithaca. But the mutiny that had been brooding was thrust forward in the form of an insolent Eurylochus, who insisted that they set down their anchors, and have a night of rest. Tiresias and Circe had warned him of this flock of sheep, and Odysseus ordered his men to touch them not, to ignore their bleatings, their succulent fat which spoke of years of grazing on tender grasses, nurtured by

Helius himself. The sailors took a solemn oath and Odysseus grudgingly allowed them to moor the ship to the rocky coast. They set about preparing a fire, and after a silent meal, fell into a deep sleep.

When morning broke, the skyline was littered with heavy clouds, tugging on the reins of a prevailing wind. And with it came a tempest which blew over the island for thirty days, prohibiting the safe voyage of the men, trapping them on an island that was empty of nourishment. And so it was that for thirty days the crew dined meagrely on corn and wine which the lovely Circe had provided, and when that was devoured, they took up their harpoons and fished the swirling waters for sustenance. And as hunger grew wild within their bodies, so did their minds wander a seditious path, along which their loyalty was cast and their oaths forgotten.

One night as Odysseus slept, weakened by hunger like his men, the errant sailors slaughtered several of Helius's sacred cows, dedicating some to the god, but gorging themselves on the carcasses of many more, till they sat, fattened and slovenly, rebelliously content. The cows were enchanted, and lowed while impaled on a spit over the fire, their empty carcasses rising to trample the ground around the men, but they repented not and continued to eat until soon their treachery was brought to the attention of Helius himself. Odysseus woke to discover the travesty and corralled his men aboard ship, urging them to escape before vengeance could be sprung upon them. But it was too late.

As Helius cried out to Zeus, imploring the king of gods to take divine retribution, Poseidon reached up his powerful staff and stirred up a tempest so violent that the ship was immediately cast to pieces in the furious waters. And Zeus sent storms and thunderbolts which broke the ship and its men into tiny pieces, crashing down the mast upon the sailors and killing them all. Only Odysseus who had remained true to the gods, was saved, and he clung to the wreckage, which formed a makeshift raft. For nine days he tumbled across waves that were larger than the fist of Poseidon himself, but his resolve was strong, his will to live was greater than the anger of the gods.

His men were drowned. Thoughts of Penelope and Telemachus kept him afloat as he fought the turbulent seas, escaping the grasp of an angry Poseidon. He was battered by the storm which drove him back to Charybdis, and as her great whirlpool was spat out, his raft was sucked into the waters that were drawn into her greedy belly. Faint with hunger, with fear, he reached out and held on to the spreading

Opposite: For seven years Odysseus lived with Calypso, drunk with luxury and love. She lived alone on her island, in a comfortable cavern hung with vines and fragrant foliage.

branches of a great fig tree and there he hung, perilously close to the vortex of water, until his raft was thrown out again. And Odysseus dropped into the sea, and paddled and drifted until he spied land once again. And only then did he allow himself to lay down his head, secure in the knowledge that help was at hand. So the noble Odysseus slept, and was washed towards the shores of this secluded island of Ogygia.

Calypso's Island

Around, thick groves their summer-dress
Wore in luxuriant loveliness —
Alder and poplar quivered there,
And fragrant cypress tower's in air.
And there broad-pinion'd birds were seen,
Nesting amid the foliage green;
Birds, which the marge of ocean hunt —
Gull, prating daw, and cormorant;
And there, the deep mouth of the cave
Fringing, the cluster'd vine-bough wave.

FROM WRANGHAM

ODYSSEUS COULD SEE LAND and in the distance a beautiful nymph, the most beautiful woman on whom he had ever laid eyes. Her milk-white skin was gleaming in the moonlight, and the wrathful winds tossed her silken hair. Her voice was soft, inviting above the raging storms.

'Come to me, Odysseus,' she whispered. 'Here you will find love, and eternal life.'

Odysseus struggled for breath, filled with longing and wonder. She reached a slender hand towards him, across the expanse of water, and lifted him from its depths, the strength of her grip, the length of her reach inhuman. He shuddered at her touch.

'You have come to join me,' she said calmly, as Odysseus laid restless and dripping beneath her.

Odysseus nodded, his passion spent. He was alive. The others had been clutched by the revengeful Poseidon. He was grateful to this nymph. He would plan his escape later.

'I have asked for you, and you have come,' she intoned quietly, settling herself at his side. Odysseus felt the first stirring of fear, but dismissed it as the lovely maiden smiled down on him.

She was Calypso, the lovely daughter of Thetis, and like Circe she was an enchantress. She lived alone on the island, in a comfortable cavern overhung by vines and fragrant foliage. She was gentle, and quiet, tending to Odysseus's every need, feeding him with morsels of delicious foods, warming him with handspun garments which clung to his body like a new skin, and she welcomed him in her bed, running his body over with hot hands that explored and relaxed the beaten hero until he grew to love her, and to build his life with her on the idyllic island.

For seven years he lived with Calypso, drunk with luxury and love. She was more beautiful than any he had seen before, and her island was dripping with pleasures. And as his happiness grew deeper, his fire and fervour spent to become a peaceful equilibrium, he felt the jab of conscience, of something untoward eating at the corners of his idyll, and he realized that he was living in a numb oblivion, that his passion to return home, to see his family, to take up the responsibilities of his leadership, were as strong in him as they had ever been and that he must allow them to surge forth, to fill him again with fiery ambition.

And in that seventh year he spent more and more time seated on the banks of the island, gazing towards his own land where time did not stand still and where his wife's suitors were threatening to take over his country, his rule. He came eventually to the notice of Athena, whose favour he had kept despite the outrage of the other gods, and she went at once to Zeus on his behalf. Zeus was fair and kind, and he balanced the sins of Odysseus against his innate good will, and the struggles to keep in check his unruly crews, all of which were lost to him now. Poseidon was away from Olympus and the time seemed right to set Odysseus free, for he had lived long enough in an enchanted purgatory.

Calypso reluctantly agreed to allow him his freedom, and she provided him with the tools to create a sturdy boat, and with provisions of food and drink enough to last the entire journey. She bathed him, dressed him in fine silks and jewels, as befitted a returning warrior, and kissing him gently but with all the fire of her love for him, she bade him go, with a tear-stained farewell. She had provided him with instructions which would see him round the dangers, across the perils that could beset him. He set sail for Ithaca.

Nausicaa and the Phaeacians

Resplendent as the moon, or solar light,
Alcinous' palace awed the o'erdazzled sight.
On to its last recess, a brazen wall
That from the threshold stretch'd, illumined all;
Round it of azure steel a cornice roll'd,
And every gate, that closed the palace, gold.
The brazen threshold golden pillars bore,
A golden ringlet glitter'd on the door,
The lintel silver, and to guard his gate,
Dogs in a row, each side, were seen to wait,
In gold and silver wrought, by Vulcan made,
Immortal as the god, and undecay'd.

SOTHEBY

WITH THE STARS of the Great Bear twinkling on his left, Odysseus sailed for eighteen days, tossed gently on a calm sea with a favourable wind breathing on the sails which were pulled tight. And then Poseidon, returning to Olympus, noticed this solitary sailor, and filled with all the fury of a wronged god, produced a calamitous wave which struck out at Odysseus and thrust him overboard. And there ensued a storm of gigantic proportions which stirred the sea into a feverish pitch which threatened with each motion to drown the terrified sailor.

But despite his many wrongs, his well-publicized shortcomings, Odysseus had made friends, and inspired awe and respect among many in Greece. And so it was that the sea-goddess Ino-Leucothea took pity on him, and swimming easily to him in the tempestuous sea, cast off his clothes and hung around his waist a magic veil, which would carry him safely to shore. She lingered before swimming away, her eyes lighting on his strong body which splashed powerfully in the waters, and she laid her hand briefly on his skin, warming him through and filling him with a deep and new energy.

Odysseus swam on, the sea calmed by Athene, and landed, exhausted on the shores of the island of the Phaeacians, where he fell into a profound slumber. Athene moved inland, into the chamber of Nausicaa, the lovely daughter of King Alcinous, and into her dreams, urging her to visit the shores of the island, to wash her clothes in the stream that tumbled by the body of the sleeping warrior. And when she woke, Nausicaa encouraged her friends to come with her to the stream, to

Opposite: Athene calmed the sea and Odysseus swam on, landing, exhausted, on the shores of the island of the Phaeacians.

play there, and to make clean her soiled garments.

Their cries of frivolity woke the sleepy Odysseus and he crawled from under a bush, naked and unruly. His wild appearance sent the friends of Nausicaa running for help, but she stood still, her virgin heart beating with anticipation. His untamed beauty inspired a carnal longing that was new to her, and from that moment she was devoted to him. She listened carefully to his words and taking his hand, led him to see her father.

Now Athene knew that King Alcinous would be less affected by Odysseus's beauty than his daughter, and prepared a healing mist which enshrouded Odysseus, who had been hastily dressed by Nausicaa.

Alcinous lived in a splendid palace, filled with glittering treasures and elegant furnishings. His table was renowned across the lands, delicious fruits soaked in fine liquors, breads veined with rich nuts, succulent meats which swirled in fine juices, glazed vegetables and herbs from the most remote gardens across the world. There were jellies and sweets, baked goods, cheeses and pâtes, fresh figs and luscious olives, all available every day to whomever visited the kind and generous leader. His women were well-versed in the vocabulary of caring for their men, and the palace gleamed with every luxury, with every necessity, to make an intelligent man content.

He listened to Odysseus now, and was struck by the power of his words. Odysseus had the appearance of a stray, but the demeanour of greatness. Alcinous wondered curiously if he was a god in disguise, so eloquent and masterful was their unknown visitor. But Odysseus kept from them his identity knowing not the reception he would receive, and careful not to destroy his chances of borrowing a ship and some men to take him to Ithaca.

And Odysseus was warmly welcomed in the palace, and fed such marvellous foods and drinks, living in such comfortable splendour, that he considered at length the request by King Alcinous and his lovely wife that he stay on to take Nausicaa as his bride. But he was too close to home to give up, and Alcinous, too polite and kind to keep Odysseus against his will, agreed to let him pass on, aided by the Phaeacian ships and hardy sailors.

So it was that on the final night of his stay with the Phaeacians he was made the guest of honour at a luxuriant feast, where the conversation turned to travels, and to war, and finally, to the victory of Troy. Inspired by their talk, a minstrel took up his lute and began to sing of the wars, of the clear skies of Ithaca, the valour of Achilles, and the skill of Odysseus and Epius. So loudly did he extol the virtues of the brave son of Laertes that Odysseus was forced to lower his head in

Opposite: Odysseus had long been thought dead, and everyone listened to tales of the illustrious hero, who had suffered such misadventures and overcome all with his cunning and mastery.

despair, and the tears fell freely to his plate where they glinted and caught the attention of the king and his men.

'Why do you suffer such dismay?' asked Alcinous gently, for he had grown fond of the elegant stranger in their midst.

Odysseus' reply was choked. The burden of the last ten years now threatened to envelope him. He had never pondered long the nature of the trials that had faced him, but as he ordered them in his mind, preparing his story to tell the King, their enormity swamped him, frightened him, made him weak.

'I am Odysseus,' he said quietly, 'son of Laertes.'

The room filled with excited joy – glasses were lifted, toasts offered, Odysseus was carried to the king where he received a long and honourable blessing. Then silence overcame them and they listened to the tales of the illustrious Odysseus who had suffered such misadventure, and overcome all with his cunning and mastery. They gazed in wonderment on the hero. He had long been thought dead, but everyone knew of the devotion, the loyalty of his wife Penelope, who refused to contemplate the idea. They encouraged him to return home. And if the unknown castaway received such glory in their generous household, a warrior of such note received the very bounty of the gods.

Ships were prepared and laden with gifts. The strongest and bravest of the Phaeacians were chosen to set sail with him, and warmed by the love and admiration of his new friends, Odysseus was placed in fine robes at the helm of a new ship, and sent towards home.

Odysseus, worn by troubles, and the relief of reaching his shores, slept deeply on board the ship, and loathe to wake him, the awe-struck sailors lifted him gently to the sands of Ithaca, where they piled his body with all the glorious gifts provided by the King, and then they retreated through the bay of Phorcys. Poseidon had been smouldering with rage at the disloyalty of Athene and Zeus, but realizing that Odysseus had been charmed, and had friends who would not allow his destruction, he allowed the hero to be placed on the sands, turning his wrath instead on the sailors. As they passed from the harbour into the seas, he struck a blow with his mighty staff and turned them all to stone, their ship frozen forever on the silent waters that led to Ithaca. It remained there as a warning to all who thought they could betray Poseidon and his mighty powers.

Opposite: Athene entered the chamber of Nausicaa, the lovely daughter of King Alcinous, and into her dreams. When she woke, Nausicaa encouraged her friends to come with her to the stream.

And so the mighty Odysseus lay once again on the shores of Ithaca, knowing not that ten years' journey had brought him at last to his promised land, or that the glory predicted by the Phaeacians would not yet be his. Battles new lined themselves on the horizon, but Odysseus was home, and from that secure base, could take on all.

❋ ❋ ❋

THE WANDERING OF ODYSSEUS
THE HOMECOMING

hen brave Odysseus was laid, deep in slumber, on the shores of Ithaca, he knew nothing of the dangers which faced his country. Loyal Penelope was ensconced in their palace, at the mercy of over a hundred suitors, rulers from neighbouring islands who wished to annex Ithaca. Telemachus had left the island in search of his father, and many of the suitors were involved in a plot to murder him upon his return. Laertes was alive, but old and troubled. When Odysseus woke, he knew not where he was. He was visited by Athene, who briefed him on the ills of his homeland, and who dressed him in the guise of a beggar, and led him to the hut of the faithful swineherd Eumaeus. Here Odysseus could plot, and plan, prepare the tools of battle to make Ithaca his once more.

Penelope and Telemachus

We wooed the wife of Odysseus, the lord so long away,
And unto that loathly wedding said she neither yea nor nay,
But the black doom and the deathday devised for us the while;
Yea in our heart she devised us moreover this same guide;
With a web that was great and mighty her loom in the house did she gear,
A fine web, full of measure, and thus bespake us there.

WILLIAM MORRIS

WHEN ODYSSEUS AWOKE on the sands of Ithaca, a mist had fallen over the majestic land and he knew not where he was. The Phaeacians had vanished from his sight, and he had only a groggy but pleasant memory of his visit to them. He should be at Ithaca now, he thought, but he could see nothing in the steamy air that enshrouded him. From the mists he heard a soft voice – familiar to Odysseus, but he no longer trusted in anything, and he sat back cautiously.

'You are in the land of the great warrior and traveller Odysseus,' said the voice, which belonged to a young and comely shepherd. 'How do you not know it?'

Odysseus lied glibly about his reasons for being there, inventing a fantastic story that was quite different from his actual voyage. At this the shepherd laughed, and changing shape, became Athene.

'So, crafty Odysseus,' she smiled. 'What a rogue you are. The greatest gods would have trouble inventing such tricks.' With that she held out a hand to the weary traveller, and led him across the sands.

'I've hidden you from your countrymen,' she explained, indicating the mists which surrounded them. 'Things are not as you would have hoped. It is not safe for you now. You must tread slowly.'

She helped Odysseus to hide away his treasures, and sat him down to explain to him the matters of his homeland. Penelope was still faithful to him, but time was running out, and she knew that if he did not appear to her within the next months, Penelope would have little recourse but to join herself with another. Telemachus was greatly angered by the insolent suitors who banded themselves at the palace, taking as their own everything that had belonged to his father, and gorging themselves on the food meant for the people of Ithaca. It was an untidy situation, and Telemachus struggled to believe that his father was still alive.

He had left the island for the mainland, desperate for news of Odysseus, never believing that his father could be dead. He'd vowed to allow one year for news, failing which he would agree to the wishes of a stepfather and stand aside.

In Greece Telemachus was greeted with little interest, and his attempts to uncover the whereabouts of his father were useless. Old Nestor, who knew everything about the war at Troy, and had followed the lives of the great men who had made the victory there, had heard nothing of Odysseus. He had disappeared, he said sadly, shaking his head. Determined, Telemachus pressed on to Sparta where Helen welcomed the son of Odysseus, but had little news to impart. Telemachus began to feel the first stirrings of despair, and sat with his head pressed into his hands. When Menelaus returned to his home that evening, he found Telemachus like this, and leaning over the youth, whispered words of comfort.

'I too have wandered,' he said gently.' And news of your father has reached me through the minions of Poseidon.' He went on to warn Telemachus of Poseidon's rage, explaining how Odysseus had blinded his one-eyed son Polyphemus. Menelaus told how Odysseus had been cast upon the shores of Calypso, where he lived a life that was half enchantment and half longing for his past.

Telemachus moved swiftly. His father was alive. A rescue must be planned at once, but most importantly he must warn his mother. The suitors had moved in too closely. They must be disposed of immediately.

At home in Ithaca, Penelope was also filled with a despair that threatened to destroy her. Her loyalty to Odysseus had kept her sane, and filled her with a kind of clever glee which made possible the machinations of keeping the suitors at bay. She'd held her head low with humility, and explained to the suitors who continued to arrive, to take roost in her home, that she must complete work on a cloth she was weaving, before she could contemplate giving herself to another. She worked hours on end in the days, performing for the suitors at her loom, giving them every belief in her excuses for not receiving their attentions. And yet at night she returned to her lonely bedroom and there she sat by torchlight, unpicking the work of the day. And as the years went by, it became established knowledge that Penelope was not free to marry until she had finished her web.

But Penelope was aware that her excuse was wearing thin, that the seeds of suspicion had been sown in the minds of her suitors, and that they were paying inordinate interest in the mechanics of the loom itself. It was

only a question of time before they would insist on her hand and she would be forced to make a choice. Her property was being wasted, her lands falling to ruin, her stocks emptied by their marauding parties. She longed for the firm hand of Odysseus to oust them from their adopted home, to renew the sense of vigour that was required by her workers to make things right again. Most importantly, however, she longed for the warm embrace of her husband, the nights of passion, of sweet love. She had resisted the attentions of her suitors, but her body was afire with longing, and she burned at a single look, at a fleeting touch. Penelope was ready for her husband's return. Soon it would be too late.

At the cottage of Eumaeus, Odysseus had been presented with a fine feast of suckling pig by the swineherd, who spoke sadly of his master's absence. He bemoaned the state of the island and explained to Odysseus in his disguise that the suitors visited his cottage regularly, taking their pick of the pigs so that his herd was sorely depleted. He said kindly that a beggarman was as entitled to a feast as were these inappropriate suitors, and he gave Odysseus his own cloak in which to warm himself by the fire. Odysseus told the loyal subject a wild story, but did say that he had heard news of Odysseus and that the great warrior would return to set his house in order within the next year. At this, the swineherd was filled with joy, and produced more food and wine for this bearer of good news. Odysseus settled in for the night.

By this time Telemachus had returned to the island, aided by Athene who had set out to greet him. He was taken to the cottage in darkness, so as not to arouse the suspicions of the suitors, who were plotting his death. Here a tearful reunion was made, away from the eyes of the swineherd who had been sent to the palace for more drink. Odysseus was transformed once more into his old self by Athene, and Telemachus drank in the sight of his father, who he'd hardly known as a child.

They sat together, heads touching, occasionally reaching over to reassure themselves of the other's presence, and the plans were made to restore Ithaca to her former glory, to rid it of the unruly suitors, to reinstate Odysseus and Telemachus at their rightful places at her helm.

Opposite:
Penelope had resisted the attentions of her suitors but her body was afire with longing and she burned at the slightest look, a fleeting touch.

The Battle for Ithaca

Then fierce the hero o'er the threshold strode;
Stripped of his rags, he blazed out like a god.
Full in their face the lifted bow he bore
And quivered deaths, a formidable store.
Before his feet the rattling shower he threw,
And thus terrific to the suitor-crew:
'One venturous game this hand has won today,
Another, princes, yet remains to play!'

HOMER

ODYSSEUS AND TELEMACHUS were ready to set their plans into action. Just before Eumaeus returned to his cottage, Odysseus resumed the form of a beggarman and Telemachus slipped away into the night. The following morning dawned cool and clear, and Odysseus felt a renewed vigour coursing through his veins. He longed to appear in his battle garb, the strong and mighty Odysseus returned from the dead to reclaim his palace, but there was too much at stake to set a wrong foot and he knew the plans he had fixed with Telemachus must be followed to the tiniest detail.

Eumaeus accompanied Odysseus to the palace, to see if there was any work available for a willing but poverty-stricken beggar. He was greeted first by the rude and arrogant Antinous, the leader of Penelope's suitors, who had long considered himself the rightful heir to Odysseus's position within Ithaca. He gazed scathingly at Odysseus as he entered the room where the suitors lolled about on cushions, calling out to the over-burdened servants for refreshment and ever greater feasts of food.

'Who dares to trouble us?' he said lazily.

Odysseus introduced himself as a poor traveller, down on his luck after a long voyage in which his crew members had been struck down by Poseidon. To test them, Odysseus begged them for alms, but he was met by a barrage of rotten fruit, after which several of the younger suitors took

Opposite: The day dawned cool and clear, and Odysseus felt a renewed vigour coursing through his veins. He longed to appear in his battle garb ... to reclaim his palace.

turns beating him. Bruised and angry, Odysseus stood his ground, requesting menial work of any nature. And it was then that the young local beggar Irus stepped into the fray. Resenting the competition offered by Odysseus, he challenged him to a fight, at which the lazy suitors leapt to their feet, roaring at the impending carnage. For

Odysseus had taken the form of an old man, and Irus was young and strong, a beggar only because of his slothful nature.

But the roars turned to silence as Odysseus lifted his robes to show legs as muscular and powerful as the greatest of warriors, and a prowess with a sword that belonged only to the master of the house. He slayed Irus with one fell of his sword. Odysseus was cheered not by the suitors, who suspected a rival for the attentions of Penelope, and they cast him out, kicking and beating him until he howled with pain and restrained anger. He could not show his true colours yet. The time was not ripe for battle. Odysseus made his way from the waiting rooms, into the kitchen where word of his ill-treatment reached Penelope. Knowing well that gods often travelled in disguise, she sent a message that she wished this sailor to be fed and made comfortable for the night. Penelope herself wished to speak to him, for a traveller might have word of the long-lost Odysseus and she yearned for news of him.

But Odysseus claimed to be too weak to see the mistress of the house, and it was agreed that they would speak later that evening. And so it was that Odysseus slipped from his bed in the kitchen and met with his son in the great hall. Quietly they removed the armour and weapons that the suitors had idly laid to one side, piling them outside the palace gates where they were snatched away by village boys. And now, in the darkened hall, Odysseus agreed to see Penelope, who felt a surge of excitement at their meeting which startled and concerned her. Odysseus had been gone too long, she was losing control.

They met by candlelight, and safe in his disguise, Odysseus wove for Penelope a fanciful story about his travels, which had little in common with the true nature of his voyages, but left her with no doubt that the brave Odysseus was on his way home, and would soon return to set things to right. And then Odysseus heard from Penelope the trials of the last twenty years, and hung his head in shame at the thought of his many years with Calypso, and the time lost through the greed and indolence of his men.

Penelope told of the suitors who had been first quietened by her insistence that the Oracle had promised Odysseus's return, but as the years had passed, they had grown insolent and arrogant, demanding her attentions, her hand in marriage. She had fought them off, she said, by claiming to weave the cloth that would shroud Laertes upon his death, and each night she had spent many hours unpicking the day's work. And then, when this trick had been discovered, she could delay

Opposite: Odysseus slayed Irus with one fell of his sword. The suitors cast him out, kicking and beating him till he howled with pain and restrained anger.

her decision no longer and had feigned illness for many months. The next day was the Feast of Apollo and it was on this day that she had agreed to choose a husband. Penelope wept with misery, her fair face more beautiful with age and distress. Odysseus longed to take her in his arms, to warm her body and to ease her pain, but he held himself back from her, knowing that he must use his anger to feed his resolve, to rid his home of these suitors once and for all.

Penelope was grateful for the reassurance and calm understanding of this stranger, and she urged him to take a chamber for the night, sending the aged nurse Eurycleia to bathe his feet and weary legs. Eurycleia had been Odysseus's own nurse as a child, and when she saw his familiar scar, received in a youthful skirmish with a wild boar, she cried out. Odysseus grabbed her throat.

'Speak not, wise woman,' he whispered harshly, 'all will be set right at the dawn of the feast.' Eurycleia nodded, her eyes bulging with fear and concern and she gathered her skirts around her, heading for the servant's quarters.

The next day was the Feast, and the household was abuzz with activity and preparations. Odysseus took a seat amongst the suitors, strategically placed by the door, but he was jeered at and heckled until he was forced to move to a small stool. Penelope eventually appeared in their midst. The Agelaus gave her an ultimatum. Today a choice must be made. Penelope turned pleadingly to Telemachus, but he nodded his grudging consent, and she announced that a competition would take place. With that she fled to a table, and shut her eyes in despair.

Telemachus took over, producing Odysseus's great bow, and gently explaining that his mother could only consider marriage to someone the equal of his father, someone who could string the bow and shoot an arrow through the rings of twelve axes set in a row. And one by one, the suitors failed to bend the stiff bow, and disgruntled, cast it aside and sat sullenly along the walls of the hall. So it was that the beggarman was the only remaining man, and he begged a chance to test his strength against the bow. He was taunted, and insults fired at him, but he stood his ground and with the permission of Penelope, who nodded a sympathetic assent, he took the bow.

Like a man born to the act, he deftly wired the bow, and taking an arrow, he fired it straight through the rings of the axes. The room was silent. Telemachus rose and strode across to stand by his father.

'The die is cast,' said Odysseus, thrusting aside his disguise. 'And another target presents itself. Prepare to pay for your treachery.' With that he lifted his arrow and shot Antinous clear through the neck. The suitors searched with amazement for their arms and armour, and finding them gone, tried to make due with the short daggers in their belts. They launched themselves on Odysseus and his son, but the two great men fought valiantly, sending arrow after arrow, spear after spear, to their fatal mark. And when Odysseus and Telemachus grew tired, Athene flew across them in the shape of a swallow and filled them with a surge of energy, a new life that saw them through the battle to victory.

The battle won, the suitors dead, the household was now scourged for those who had befriended the suitors, maids who had shared their beds, porters and shepherds who had made available the stocks and stores of Odysseus's palace. And these maids and men were beheaded and burnt in a fire that was seen for many miles.

Finally Odysseus could pause, and greet properly his long-lost wife, who sat wearily by his side, hardly daring to believe that he had returned. And yet, one look at his time and journey-lined face told her it was all true, and she was overwhelmed once again by her love for this brave man who was so long apart from her. With tears of joy they clutched one another, and their union was sweet and tender. And soon afterwards came Laertes, the veil of madness lifted by news of his son's return.

The courageous Odysseus was home at last, his cunning a match for all that the fates had set in his path. There would be more skirmishes before he could call Ithaca his own once more, and Poseidon must be appeased before he could live fearlessly surrounded by that great god's kingdom, but in time all was undertaken. Some say that Odysseus lived to a ripe old age, dying eventually and suitably on the sea. Others say that he died at the hand of his own son, Telegonus, by the enchantress Circe. All agree that Odysseus was beloved by his subjects, the tales of his journey becoming the food for legends which spread around the world.

✳   ✳   ✳

MYTHS OF LOVE AND COURAGE

he gods and goddesses of Greece were the creators of the earth, makers of the universe and rulers thereafter. In their hectic lives, governed by deep-seated jealousies, petty hatreds, overwhelming passion and love, and desperate bids for revenge, there were other beings, mortals who led lives cast in the shadows of these greater entities. But it was also the acts of these mortals which became tools of understanding for the Greeks, for how could they make sense of the world in which they lived without the interaction of mankind with gods? From where came the echo in the deep valleys of Greece; how do you explain the powerful spirits of the woodland, the waters, the winds? These are the tales of mystery and enchantment which form some of the most exquisite allegories in literature worldwide; they speak of love, desire, deceit and trickery; they explain all.

Eros and Psyche

O brightest! though too late for antique vows,
Too, too late for the fond believing lyre,
When holy were the haunted forest boughs,
Holy the air, the water, and the fire;
Yet even in these days so far retired
From happy pieties, thy lucent fans
Fluttering among the faint Olympians,
I see, and sing, by my own eyes inspired.
So let me be thy choir, and make a moan
Upon the midnight hours;
Thy voice, thy lute, thy pipe, thy incense sweet
From singed censer teeming;
Thy shrine, thy grove, thy oracle, thy heat,
Of pale-mouthed prophet dreaming.

ODE TO PSYCHE, JOHN KEATS

ONCE THERE WAS A KING and a queen with three lovely daughters. The youngest daughter, Psyche, was so beautiful, so fair of face that she was revered throughout the land, and the subjects of her father reached out to touch her as she passed. No suitors dared to cross her doorstep, so highly was she worshiped. Psyche was deeply lonely.

Her beauty became legend, far and wide, and it was not long before word of it reached the ears of Aphrodite, the epitome of all beauty, the goddess of love herself. Tales of the young princess enraged the jealous goddess, and she made plans to dispose of her. Aphrodite arranged for Psyche's father to present Psyche as a sacrifice, in order to prevent his kingdom being devoured by a monster, and this he grudgingly did, placing her on a mountaintop, and bidding her a tearful farewell.

Eros, the errant son of Aphrodite, was sent to murder Psyche but he too was entranced by her gentle ways, and implored Zephyr, the West Wind, to lift her and place her down far from the hillside, in a lush and verdant valley. When Psyche opened her eyes, she found herself in front of a sumptuous palace unlike any she had seen before. She called out, and although there was no response, quiet voices simmered just beyond her hearing, comforting her, soothing her, setting her at ease. She stretched and thought briefly of food, at which a platter of succulent morsels was laid, as if by magic, at her disposal. When she grew tired, a soft bed was presented, and she slipped dreamlessly into sleep.

Psyche woke in the night. A presence had stirred her, but she felt no fear. A warmth pervaded the room and she closed her eyes, sinking into its musky perfume. She was joined and embraced by a body so inviting, she gave herself at once, filled by a sense of joy that overwhelmed her.

'Who are you,' she whispered, and a finger was laid firmly to her lips. She said no more, spending the night in tender love. When she woke, she felt gilded, but her bed was empty.

And so the days passed, with Psyche growing ever more peaceful, ever happier. She had clothes and jewels which miraculously appeared – her every comfort was seen to. And the only hole in her happiness was loneliness, for apart from the moonlit visits from her phantom husband, she was entirely alone. She'd tried to learn more about this man who held her each night in passionate embrace, but he'd told her that his identity must remain secret, or their alliance would be no more. She agreed to his wishes because she loved him, because he filled her with a sense of belonging that she had never before experienced.

One day, however, her peaceful idyll was interrupted by the cries of her two sisters. Concerned about her disappearance, they'd spent many weeks searching the hills, and now they stood just beyond the bend of the valley. Shrieking with delight, Psyche raced up the mountain, and drew them back into her new home. And as she toured her sisters around her exquisite palace, she failed to notice their growing silence, their churlish looks. Her sisters were sickened with envy, and they teased their younger sister about her ghostly lover.

'No,' she protested, 'he was real.' She felt him, explored him each night. Held him warm in her arms.

But her sisters taunted and teased until Psyche agreed to seek out his identity. That night, when he came to her once again, she broke her word for the first time, leaning across him to light the oil lamp. As she moved, a drop of the hot liquid fell onto the snow white skin of her lover, and his face was revealed. He was none other than the most beautiful of the gods, Eros, son of Aphrodite. But burned, and bewildered, he rose from her bed and disappeared from her forever.

Psyche's torment was so deep that she tried to take her own life. Eros, still deeply in love with his wife, but now invisible to her, saved her on each occasion, caring for her as she travelled across the kingdom in search of him. He longed to touch her, but the wrath of his mother was more than he could bear. He longed to speak to her, but could use only the trees, the winds, the creatures of the forest, to deliver his words.

Searching far and wide for Eros, Psyche came, by and by, to the home of Aphrodite. Poisoned by her jealousy, Aphrodite resolved to dispose of the young princess, knowing not of her son's attachment, caring only that Psyche was more beautiful than she, and that Psyche had eluded her careful plot to send her to her death. She set the young princess impossible tasks, determined to punish her further.

The first task was to pluck the golden wool from a flock of blood-thirsty sheep. As Psyche stood by the edge of their paddock, she heard the quiet song of the reeds in the wind. As she listened, their words became clear. She was not to pluck the wool from their backs. There, on the gorsebushes which lined their field, was the wool that had been brushed from their hides each time they passed. She crept over and filled her basket. Gleefully she returned to Aphrodite, basket held high, but her mistress's sour expression greeted her, and all hope of freedom vanished.

The goddess sent her out once again, this time to fetch water from the stream which flowed to the Styx, the river of the Underworld. As she neared its banks, Psyche grew frightened. The stream itself cut through a deep gorge, and all her efforts to reach its waters failed. Furthermore, as she caught a glimpse of its shimmering blackness, she became aware of the guard of dragons, who patrolled its shores, boiling the seething waters with their fiery breath. She sank down in despair, her bottle falling to her side.

Suddenly it was snatched up, and into the air, clutched in the grasp of Zeus's Royal Eagle. The winds had told him of Psyche's plight, and enchanted by her loveliness, he vowed to help her. Smoothly he dodged the dragons, filling the flask and returning it to her waiting arms.

Aphrodite was ill pleased by this success. She had imagined Psyche long dead by now, and set all her powers of determination to plot the third task. Psyche was to descend to the Afterworld, and beg Persephone for some of her beauty, which should be returned to Aphrodite. Once again Psyche tried to take her own life, deep in desolation and longing for Eros, and frustrated by the seemingly impossible tasks before her. But yet again, she was plucked from death by Eros, and through his powers realized the way to achieve her task. The tower from which she had attempted to leap confirmed the instructions.

Psyche was to follow the path nearby, which would take her to the Afterworld. She was to take several things along – barley cakes and

Opposite: Zeus examined the goodness of Psyche, her dedication and her exquisite charms. He agreed to allow her marriage to Eros, he agreed to make her immortal.

honey cakes for Cerberus, the three-headed dog who guarded the entry and two coins to pay Charon, the ferryman. She was to ignore the messages of her own kind heart and refuse help to anyone who sought her assistance along the way.

Psyche set off, the words ringing in her ears. As she journeyed she was met by hapless travellers who called out for her help. At every turn lay another trap set by Aphrodite, who was determined for Psyche to remain in the Afterworld once and for all. But Psyche too had determination, fed by love for Eros, to whom she longed to return. She made her way past the pitfalls set out for her, and on to Persephone, who presented her with a box.

As she returned once more to the land of the living, she was struck by curiosity, and opened the box. The box seemed empty. But as she struggled to close it, she felt an overwhelming sleep flower around her, kissing shut her eyes, and drawing from her lungs her final breath. Death clung to the maiden, embracing her lifelessness, waiting for its usurpation to be complete.

Ever vigilant, Eros flew down, brushing the sleep of death from her eyes and placing it back in the box. And so Psyche was revived, fresh and invigorated, and glowing with new life. She returned to Aphrodite, and handed over the deadly box. She waited with anticipation. Surely Aphrodite was finished with her now.

But the goddess had a final task in store for Psyche, and led her to a large shed, full of various grains. Here lay oats, and black beans, millet, lentils, vetch and poppyseeds, wheat and rye, mixed together in an overwhelming pile. Psyche was to sort it, said Aphrodite firmly. And then she could be free.

Psyche crouched down and gingerly picked at the pile. Tears welled in her eyes and she felt the beginnings of despair touching again at her heart. As the first glistening tear fell, a tiny voice woke her from her sorrow. An ant, enchanted by the lovely princess, had moved to her side. He could help, he said, and so it was that hundreds of ants marched to the pile, and within just one hour the pile was sorted.

Aphrodite was enraged, but she was also wise enough to know that Psyche was not going to succumb to her plots. She set her free, and Psyche set off once more in her search for Eros.

Now Eros had been deeply disillusioned by his mother's antics. Her jealousy had sparked in him a rebellion such as he'd never felt before, and with a revelatory burst, he flew at once to Olympus and begged Zeus to offer his advice.

Zeus was the King of gods for many reasons. Throughout his reign, many such sensitive matters were put before him, and his awesome wisdom and sense of justice had always prevailed. On this day, Eros was not disappointed. Zeus examined the goodness of Psyche, her dedication and her exquisite charms. He agreed to allow her marriage to Eros, he agreed to make her immortal. And in return Eros must become reconciled to his mother, and they must share the deep respect of family.

And so it was that Psyche became a daughter to Aphrodite, and entered a union with Eros. She returned once again to her palace in the valley, to a happiness that was enriched by the goodness in her heart and which was, as a result of her tribulations, now complete.

The Rape of Persephone

... that fair field
Of Enna, where Proserpine, gathering flowers,
Herself a fairer flower, by gloomy Dis
Was gathered, which cost Ceres all that pain
To seek her through the world ...

PARADISE LOST, JOHN MILTON

PERSEPHONE WAS THE DAUGHTER of Zeus and Demeter, a virgin of such remarkable beauty that she was kept hidden from the eyes of wishful suitors for all of her life. She spent her days idyllically, gathering fragrant flowers in the fields which spread as far as the eye could see, and dancing with the wood folk, who doted on the young maiden. Demeter was goddess of the earth, and Persephone whiled away the long summery hours helping her mother to gather seeds, to pollinate, and to sow the fertile earth. She was shielded from the outside world by her doting parents, kept carefully away from the dangers that could befall so fair a creature. They lived in the Vale of Enna, where Persephone blossomed like the flowers which surrounded her sanctuary.

One warm, sun-kissed evening, Persephone lay back in the long grasses by the idle stream which trickled through the paddock at the end of the garden. Bees hummed above the lapping waters, butterflies glided and came to rest beside the serene young woman. An eager toad lapped at the darting dragonflies. Persephone's beauty was accentuated by lush green grass, and by the expression of placid contentment which embraced her exquisite features.

It was no wonder then, that the passionate Hades, king of the Underworld, should stop in his tracks when he spied this graceful vision, should draw back the anarchic horses which lunged and tugged at his fiery chariot. He drew a deep breath. He must have her.

Now Hades and Zeus were brothers, and Hades thought nothing of approaching him to ask for Persephone's hand in marriage. Zeus knew that his daughter would be well cared for by Hades, but he felt saddened by the thought of losing her to the world from which no mortal could return. He wavered, reluctant to displease his brother, but more apprehensive still of the wrath of Demeter, who would never allow such a match to take place. Zeus announced that he could not offer his permission, but neither would he deny it, and encouraged by this response, Hades returned to the peaceful spot where Persephone lay and seized her. A great chasm opened in the earth, and holding Persephone under an arm, Hades and his horses plunged into the dark world beneath.

It was many hours before Demeter realized that Persephone had vanished, and many days before she could come to terms with her loss. She shunned the attentions of Zeus, refused to attend the council of the gods. She dressed herself in the robes of a beggarwoman, and in this disguise, prepared to roam the realm, in search of her missing daughter. The earth grew bare as Demeter ceased to tend it; fruit withered on the vine, plenteous fields grew fallow, the warm western winds ceased to blow. The land grew cold and barren.

Demeter's travels took her across many lands. At each, she stopped, searched, and begged for information. At each she was turned away empty-handed, often snubbed and ill-treated. She grew colder, and famine spread across the earth. At last she came to the land of Eleusis, the kingdom of Celeus and his wife Metaneira. There Demeter, in her disguise, was welcomed and taken in by Queen Metaneira, who instinctively trusted the beggarwoman and asked her to act as nurse to her baby son, the Prince Demaphoon.

Demeter was weakened by her journey, and welcomed the respite. She fell in love with the young prince, and poured out her longing for her daughter in his care. She grew more content, bathing the infant in nectar and holding him daily above the fire in order to burn away his mortality. The greatest gift she could offer him was immortality, and she poured her supreme powers into the process, protecting the child from the flames so that he remained unharmed.

Opposite: Persephone's beauty was accentuated by the lush green grass and by the expression of placid contentment which embraced her exquisite features.

One day, Metaneira paid an unexpected visit to the nursery, and chanced to see this extraordinary sight. She flew into a panic, and the startled Demeter dropped the child in to the fire, where he was burned to death. At once Demeter took on her godly form, and chastised the Queen for causing the death of the child they both loved so deeply. The people of Eleusis paid tribute to the god in their midst, and in return she set up a temple, and showed them how to plant and sow seeds in the arid earth. She blessed them, and as their kindness was repaid by an end to their years of famine, so came the news she had long awaited.

A stranger came to her in her temple one night, as she prepared to retire. He'd been tending his flocks, he said, and he'd seen the ground open up to greet a flaming chariot led by a team of black horses. In the carriage was a screaming girl who'd thrust something into the startled herder's hands, just before the earth closed upon her. He held it out to her now. It was Persephone's girdle.

The wretched Demeter knew at once what had befallen her beloved precious daughter. She returned in haste to Olympus, where she confronted Zeus. And so it was decided that Persephone should be allowed to return to her mother. He sent word to Hades, who reluctantly agreed to part from his young bride. As Persephone prepared to leave, he shyly offered her a pomegranate to eat on the journey, a token of his love, his esteem, he said. Persephone was charmed by the gesture, and breaking the fast she had undertaken while trapped in the Underworld, she nibbled at several seeds.

At once darkness fell upon her. Her mother stood just past the gates to the Underworld, but she was unable to reach her. For any mortal who eats or drinks in the land of Hades has no choice but to remain there forever. A chasm opened between mother and child, one which neither could pass.

But Zeus, ashamed by his part in the matter, and deeply concerned by Demeter's neglect of the land, which refused to flower or bear fruit, stepped in. It was agreed that Persephone would become reunited with her mother, and make her home again on earth. But for three months each year, one month for every seed of the pomegranate she had eaten, she must return to the underworld, and become Hades' queen.

Their reunion was warmed by the sun, which shone for the first time on the cold land. Birds poked their heads from knotted branches, buds and then leaves thrust their way through the hardened earth. Spring had arrived in all her fecund splendour.

But for the three months each year in which Persephone returns to Hades, Demeter throws her cloak across the earth, bringing sterility and darkness until Persephone breathes once more in the land of the living, bringing Spring.

Orpheus and Eurydice

Heavenly o'er the startled Hell,
Holy, where the Accursed dwell,
O Thracian, went thy silver song!
Grim Minos with unconscious tears,
Melts into mercy as he hears –
The serpents in Megaera's hair
Kiss, as they wreathe enamoured there;
All harmless rests the madding throng;–
From the torn breast the Vulture mute
Flies, scared before the charmed lute–
Lulled into sighing from their roar
The dark waves woo the listening shore–
Listening the Thracian's silver song!–
Love was the Thracian's silver song!

JOHANN CHRISTOPH FRIEDRICH VON SCHILLER

THE MUSIC OF ORPHEUS was known across the lands. With his lyre, he played the sweetest strains which lulled even the fiercest beasts into a peaceful rapture. For his music Orpheus was loved, and he travelled far and wide, issuing forth melodies that were pure, sublime.

Orpheus was the son of Apollo and the muse Calliope. He lived in Thrace and spent his days singing, playing the music that spread his fame still further. One day, Orpheus came across a gentle and very beautiful young nymph, who danced to his music as if she was born to do so. She was called Eurydice, and wings seemed to lift her heels, as she played and frolicked to his music. And then, when their eyes caught, it was clear that it was love at first sight and that their destiny was to be shared.

It was only a few days later that they were joined in marriage, and never before had such an angelic couple existed. As they danced on the eve of their wedding, the very trees and flowers, the winds and rushing streams paused and then shouted their congratulations. The world stopped to watch, to approve, to celebrate.

And then that most sinister of animals, a stealthy viper, made its way into the babbling midst and struck at the ankle of Eurydice, sending her to an icy, instant death. Eurydice sank down in the circle, and all efforts to revive her failed. Time seemed to stop. Certainly there was no music, anywhere.

Orpheus was disconsolate with grief. He could not even bring himself to bury her, and he played on his lyre such tunes that even the rocks, the hardened fabric of the caves, shed tears. After several days he came to a decision which seemed at once as clear and as necessary as anything he had ever undertaken.

Orpheus made his way to the Underworld, determined to rescue his great love. His lyre in hand, his heart pounding with emotion, he reached the river Styx, the black waterway which snakes its way into the underworld, which divides the other world from our own. There he played his lute so tunefully, so eloquently, that Charon, the ferryman, took him across the river at no charge, granted access to a place into which no mortal must go.

As Orpheus was drawn deeper into the Underworld, grisly, frightening sights greeted his eyes, but he continued to play his soulful tune, filling with tears the eyes of those cast in wretched purgatory, the ghosts of beings who had done ill deeds, the spirits of men who had been cursed. He played on and on, his music seeping into the blackness and creating an effortless light which guided the way.

At the end of his journey King Hades and Queen Persephone sat, entranced by his music. They knew of his mission. They would allow him to take Eurydice. His music had unwound the rigours of their rules, of their laws, and momentarily appeased, temporarily relaxed, they permitted Orpheus to take one of their own.

There was a condition, as there is in all such matters. Orpheus could have his bride returned to him; she would follow him as his shadow. But he must not look back on his trip from their world. The music from Orpheus' lyre picked up the timbre of his pleasure and took on a jaunty character which brought a look of surprise to the stony faces of Hades'

Opposite: With his lyre, Orpheus played the sweetest strains which lulled even the fiercest beasts into peaceful rapture.

guards. Orpheus turned and made his way back to the Styx, to his world, to home and Eurydice.

The gate of the Underworld was in sight when Orpheus felt an overwhelming need to confirm that Eurydice was there. Instinctively,

he turned towards his great love, and there she stood, shrouded in a dark cape. As he reached for her, just as he felt the warmth of her skin, her breath on his cheek, she vanished, drawn back into death, into the darkened world of the afterlife.

Orpheus left the Underworld alone, and when he returned to his land, he lay broken and wasted on the shores of the Styx. For the rest of his short life he wandered among the hills, carrying a broken lyre which he would not mend and could not play. He cared for nothing. He was attacked, one day, without the powers to play, to appease his enemy. His attackers were a throng of Thracian women who killed him, and tore him to pieces. His lyre was taken to Lesbos, where it became a shrine, and some years later, his head was washed upon the shores of the island. There it was joined with his sacred lyre, its broken strings representing forever the broken heart of Orpheus.

Echo and Narcissus

Pan loved his neightbour Echo – but that child
Of Earth and Air pined for the Satyr leaping;
The Satyr loved with wasting madness wild
The bright nymph Lyda, – and so three went weeping:
As Pan loved Echo, Echo loved the Satyr,
The Satyr, Lyda – and thus love consumed them.
And thus to each – which was a woeful matter –
To bear what they inflicted, justice doom'd them;
For inasmuch as each might hate the lover,
Each loving, so was hated. – Ye that love not
Be warn'd – in thought turn this example over,
That when ye love, the like return ye prove not.

MOCHUS, TRANSLATED BY PERCY BYSSHE SHELLEY

ECHO WAS A WOOD NYMPH who danced and sang in the forest. She told engaging stories to anyone who would listen, and although she was adored by the other nymphs her headstrong ways meant that none of her playmates had the last word. Echo would skip and frolic among the trees, charming the small creatures and befriending the forest folk as she played.

Hera was enchanted by the nubile young nymph, and she came

Opposite:
Echo had been drawn to Narcissus for many months and secretly followed him in the forest, begging him silently to speak.

daily to hear Echo's tales of adventure, of fairies and of far-off places, stories that grew ever more complicated with each telling. One day Hera left earlier than usual, inspired to see her husband Zeus by Echo's romantic tales. It was on this day that Hera was presented with evidence of her husband's philanderings, and discovered that Echo had been involved in the subterfuge, receiving a wage from Zeus to occupy his lovely wife.

Hera flew into a rage which resounded through the Kingdom, and the victim of her wrath was Echo, who was stripped of her power of speech, able only to echo the last words spoken by any person. Echo fled deep into the forest, tortured by her speechlessness, drained of her life and vitality.

Now in this same forest lived a handsome young man named Narcissus, a Thespian and the son of the blue nymph Leirope and the River-god Cephisus. When Narcissus was but a child, his mother consulted the seer Tiresias to learn of his fortune. Would he live to old age? she longed to know.

'If he never knows himself,' said the wise man.

Tales of Narcissus' beauty had spread far and wide and it was not long before a he grew conceited and self-satisfied. Lovers came and went, but Narcissus' heart grew colder, frosted by the knowledge that none could match his charm and grace.

Echo had been drawn to the youth for many months, and secretly followed him in the forest, begging him silently to speak so she could make her presence known. One day her wish was granted, and Narcissus, who had lost his companions in the forest, called out, 'Is anyone here?"

'Here,' cried the young nymph with delight.

'Come!' replied Narcissus, his face a haughty mask.

'Come!' repeated Echo.

'Why do you avoid me?' asked Narcissus, a surprised look crossing his face.

'Why do you avoid me?' said Echo.

'Let us come together,' he shouted, with careless confidence. He looked purposefully around, his manly brow furrowed with intrigue.

'Let us come together.' And as the words tumbled from Echo's tender lips, she leapt from her hiding place, and threw herself against the comely young man.

He stepped back in horror, roughly detaching himself from her grasp, and snarling, 'I will die before you ever lay with me!' Summoning up the arrogance of his youth, he cast Echo aside and left

Opposite: As Narcissus leant over the crystal waters he was caught by a sight of such beauty that his breath escaped in a stunned gasp.

the clearing, failing to hear her pleading 'Lay with me ...' as he stalked away.

Echo grew cold with misery, and unable to draw breath, she lay still and pined for her lost love, the vessel for her childish hopes and aspirations. There Echo laid until she was no more than her voice, her tiny body becoming one with the woodland floor.

Narcissus quickly forgot this uneasy encounter, and carried on his relentless search for love. One day, deep in the forest, he stopped his hunting in order to take a drink from a pure, clear stream. As he leant over the crystal waters he was caught by such a sight of beauty that his breath escaped in a stunned gasp. There, in this magical current, was a face of such perfect loveliness that Narcissus was unable to move, to call out.

He whispered to the dazzling illusion, but though the lips of this creature moved, too, no sound was uttered. Narcissus was enchanted. He reached forwards to the elegant face, the princely features, but alas, with every movement the object of his passion disappeared in a kaleidoscope of colour.

Narcissus had fallen in love with his own reflection, and he was held captive by its magnificence. He reclined by the stream, unable to move, and there he laid without food or water until he too pined away, to become one with the forest. The last words to slip from his aristocratic lips were, 'O youth beloved in vain. Farewell.' To which the spirit of the love-sickened nymph Echo replied, 'Farewell.'

Those who had once swooned for Narcissus prepared his funeral

pyre, but his body had disappeared. In its place grew a slim and elegant flower with a blood-red heart, which gazed piteously at its reflection as it dipped over the water. Today, this flower can be found by the waters of certain streams, a flower known for its beauty, which gazes eternally at its own reflection.

The spirit of Echo is often heard, for she fled that forest, and wanders far from the shores of that stream, ever searching for her lost love, and, of course, her voice.

Perseus and the Gorgon

Peaceful grew the land
The while the ivory rod was in his hand,
For robbers fled, and good men still waxed strong,
And in no house was any sound of wrong,
Until the Golden Age there seemed to be,
So steeped the land was in felicity.

WILLIAM MORRIS

THERE ONCE WAS A TROUBLED KING who learned, through an Oracle, that he would reach his death through the hand of his own grandson. This king was Acrisius, king of Argos, and he had only one child, the fair Danae. Acrisius shut her away in a cave, in order to keep her unwedded, and there she grew older, and more beautiful, as time passed. No man could reach her, although many tried, and eventually word of her beauty reached the gods, and finally the king of the Gods himself, Zeus.

He entered her prison in a cascade of light, and planted in her womb the seed of the gods, and from this the infant Perseus was spawned. Acrisius heard the infant's cries, and unable to kill him outright, he released Danae from her prison, and with her child she was placed on a raft, and sent out on the stormy seas to meet their death.

Now Poseidon knew of Zeus's child, and calmed the seas, lifting the mother and child carefully to the island of Seriphos, where they washed onto safe shores. They were discovered there by a kind fisherman, who brought them to his home. It was in this humble and peaceful abode that Perseus grew up, a boy of effortless intelligence, cunning and nobility. He was a sportsman beyond compare, and a

Opposite:
Narcissus had fallen in love with his own reflection. He was held captive by its magnificence. He reclined by the stream unable to move.

hero among his playmates. He was visited in his dreams by Athene, the goddess of war, who filled his head with lusty ambition and inspired him to seek danger and excitement.

The fisherman became a father figure to Perseus, but another schemed to take his place. The fisherman's brother Polydectes, chief of the island, was besotted by the beautiful Danae, and longed to have her for his wife. He showered her with priceless jewels, succulent morsels of food, rich fabrics and furs, but her heart belonged to Perseus, and she refused his attentions. Embittered, he resolved to dispose of the youth, and set Perseus a task at which he could not help but fail, and from which no mortal man could ever return.

The task was to slay the creature Medusa, one of the three Gorgon sisters. Medusa was the only mortal of the Gorgons, with a face so hideous, so repulsive, that any man who laid eyes on her would be turned to stone before he could attack. Her hair was a nest of vipers, which writhed around that flawed and fatal face. Perseus was enthralled by the idea of performing an act of such bravery and that night, as he slept, he summoned again the goddess Athene, who provided him with the tools by which the task could be shouldered.

Athene came to him, a glorious figure of war, and with her she brought Hermes, her brother, who offered the young man powerful charms with which he could make his way. Perseus was provided with Hermes own crooked sword, sturdy enough to cut through even the strongest armour, and Perseus's feet were fitted with winged sandals, by which he could make his escape. From Pluto he received a helmet which had the power to make its wearer invisible. Athene offered her mirrored shield, which would allow Perseus to strike Medusa without seeing her horrible face. Finally, he was given a skin bag, to carry the Gorgon's head from the site.

Perseus set out the next morning, his first assignment to find the half-sisters of the Gorgons, in the icy wilderness of the northern steppes of Graiae. They alone could provide him with the whereabouts of Medusa. With the aid of his winged sandals, Perseus flew north, till he came to the frosted mists of the mountains. There the earth was so cold, a fabulous crack was rent across her surface. The land was barren, icy, empty, and although he felt no fear, Perseus had to struggle to carry on, his breath frozen on his lips. There, on the edge of the Hyperborean sea were the Gray Sisters, witches from another era who had come there to end their days, wreaking a wretched existence from

Opposite: The Gorgons were not human and could not, like Medusa, be slain by humans. They rose on wings, like murderous vultures, yowling and gnashing their teeth.

the snow-capped mountains, toothless and haggard with age. They had but one eye between them, and one tooth, without which they would surely have died.

Perseus chose his moment carefully, and lunged into their midst, grasping their single eye, and stepping out of reach.

'I require your assistance,' he said firmly. 'I must know the way to the Gorgons. If you cannot help me I shall take your tooth as well, and you shall starve in this wilderness.'

The Gray Sisters swayed and muttered, lolling upon the snow and fumbling across its icy surface towards the awe-inspiring voice.

A cry rose up when they realized that he had their eye, and they threatened and cursed Perseus, their howls echoing in the blackness of the wasteland. Finally, they succumbed, the fear of blindness in that empty place enlivening their tongues, loosening their resolve. Perseus graciously returned their eye, and on a breath of Arctic air, he rose and headed southwards, out of sight of the sisters, who struggled to see their tormentor.

Back through the mists he flew, where the sea sent spirals of spray that lashed at his heels and tried to drag him down. On he went, and the snows melted away into a sea so blue he seemed enveloped in it. The sky grew bright, the grass of the fields green and inviting, and as he flew he grew hotter, his eyes heavy with exhaustion, his perfect skin dripping with effort. The other end of the world rose up, a land and a sea where no human dared enter, a land of burning heat, of fiery hatred and fear, where none lived but the Gorgons themselves, surrounded by the hapless stone statues of man and beast who had dared to look upon them.

He came across the sisters as they slept in the midday sun. Medusa lay between her sisters, who protectively laid their arms across her mass. Her body was scaled and repellent, her limbs clawed and gnarled. Perseus dared look no further, but from the corner of his eye he saw the coiling vipers, and the serpent's tongue which even in sleep darted from her razor-sharp lips. Her fearsome eyes were shut. He was safe.

With one decisive movement he plunged himself and his sword towards this creature, Athene's shield held high. And Medusa's answering howl pierced the air, ripping the breath from his lungs, and dragging him down towards her. He struggled to maintain his composure, shivering and drawn to look at the source of this violent cry. He fell on her, shaking his head to clear it, fighting the temptation to give in. And then the courage that was deep inside him, born within him, the gift of his father Zeus, redeemed him. He lifted his head, and with shield held high, thrust his sword in one wild swoop that lopped off the head of Medusa.

He packed it hastily in his bag, and leapt up, away from the arms of the Sisters Gorgon who had woken abruptly, and now hissed and struck out at him. The Gorgons were not human, and could not, like Medusa, be slain by humans. They rose on wings, like murderous vultures, yowling and gnashing their teeth, screaming of revenge.

But Perseus had disappeared.

His helmet took him from their side, enshrouded him with a curtain that protected him from their eyes. He was safe.

For days on end he flew with his booty, across the desert, where the dripping blood of Medusa hit the sand and bred evil vipers and venomous snakes, ever to populate the sunburnt earth. The Gorgons flew behind him, a whirlwind of hatred and revenge, but Perseus soared above them, until he was safe, at the edge of his world.

He came to rest at the home of Atlas, the giant, who held up with great pillars the weight of the sky. He begged for a place to lay his weary head, for sustenance and water. But the giant refused him. Tired and angry, Perseus thrust his hand into his bag and drew out the monstrous head. To this day, Atlas stands, a stone giant holding up the skies, his head frosted with snow, his face frozen with horror.

And Perseus flew on, although it was several months and many more challenges before he was able to present his trophy. But his travels are another story, involving passion, bravery and an ultimate battle. He would meet Polydectes once again, would defend his hostage mother, and face his long-lost grandfather. He would make his own mark at Olympus, and become, eventually, a bright star, a divine beacon which would guide courageous wanderers, as he had once been.

✻ ✻ ✻

GLOSSARY

Achilles	The son of Peleus and the sea-nymph Thetis, who distinguished himself in the Trojan War. He was made almost immortal by his mother, who dipped him in the River Styx and he was invincible except for a portion of his heel which remained out of the water.
Acropolis	Citadel in a Greek city.
Aeneas	The son of Anchises and the goddess Aphrodite, reared by a nymph. He led the Dardanian troops in the Trojan War. According to legend,he became the founder of Rome.
Agamemnon	A famous King of Mycenae. He married Helen of Sparta's sister Clytemnestra. When Paris abducted Helen, beginning the Trojan War, Menelaus called on Agamemnon to raise the Greek troops. He had to sacrifice his daughter Iphigenia in order to get a fair wind to travel to Troy.
Agora	Greek marketplace.
Ajax	Ajax the Greater was the bravest, after Achilles, of all warriors at Troy, fighting Hector in single combat and distinguishing himself in the Battle of the Ships. He was not chosen as the bravest warrior and eventually went mad.
Ajax	Ajax of Locri was another warrior at Troy. When Troy was captured he committed the ultimate sacrilege by seizing Cassandra from her sanctuary with the Palladium.
Alcinous	King of the Phaeacians.
Ambrosia	Food of the gods.
Apollo	One of the twelve Olympian gods, son of Zeus and Leto. He is attributed with being the god of plague, music, song and prophecy.
Arachne	A Lydian woman with great skill in weaving. She was challenged in a competition by the jealous Athene who destroyed her work and when she killed herself, turned her into a spider destined to weave until eternity.
Ares	God of War, 'gold-changer of corpses', and the son of Zeus and Hera.
Argonauts	Heroes who sailed with Jason on the ship Argo to fetch the golden fleece from Colchis.
Artemis	The virgin goddess of the chase, attributed with being the moon goddess and the primitive mother-goddess. She was daughter of Zeus and Leto.
Asclepius	God of healing who often took the form of a snake. He is the son of Apollo by Coronis.
Asopus	The god of the River Asopus.
Athene	Virgin warrior-goddess, born from the forehead of Zeus when he swallowed his wife Metis. Plays a key role in the travels of Odysseus, and Perseus.
Augeas	King of Elis, one of the Argonauts.
Britomartis	A Cretan goddess, also known as Dictynna.
Calchas	The seer of Mycenae who accompanied the Greek fleet to Troy. It was his prophecy which stated that Troy would never be taken without the aid of Achilles.
Calypso	A nymph who lived on the island of Ogygia.
Cerberus	The three-headed dog who guarded the entrance to the Underworld.
Charon	The ferryman of the dead who carries souls across the River Styx to Hades.
Charybdis	See Scylla and Charybdis.
Chrysaor	Son of Poseidon and Medusa, born from the severed neck of Medusa when Perseus beheaded her.
Chryseis	Daughter of Chryses who was taken by Agamemnon in the battle of Troy.
Circe	An enchantress and the daughter of Helius. She lived on the island of Aeaea with the power to change men to beasts.
Cleobis and Biton	Two men of Argos who dragged the wagon carrying their mother, priestess of Hera, from Argos to the sanctuary.
Clio	Muse of history and prophecy.

Clytemnestra	Daughter of Tyndareus, sister of Helen, who married Agamemnon but deserted him when he sacrificed Iphigenia, their daughter, at the beginning of the Trojan War.
Cyclopes	One-eyed giants who were imprisoned in Tartarus by Uranus and Cronus, but released by Zeus, for whom they made thunderbolts. Also a tribe of pastoralists who live without laws, and on, whenever possible, human flesh.
Daedalus	Descendant of the Athenian King Erechtheus and son of Eupalamus. He killed his nephew and apprentice. Famed for constructing the labyrinth to house the Minotaur, in which he was later imprisoned. He constructed wings for himself and his son to make their escape.
Danae	Daughter of Acrisius, King of Argos. Acrisius trapped her in a cave when he was warned that his grandson would be the cause of his ultimate death. Zeus came to her and Perseus was born.
Danaids	The fifty daughters of Danaus of Argos, by ten mothers.
Dardanus	Son of Zeus and Electra, daughter of Atlas.
Deianeira	Daughter of Oeneus, who married Heracles after he won her in a battle with the River Achelous.
Demeter	Goddess of agriculture and nutrition, whose name means earth mother. She is the mother of Persephone.
Demophoon	Son of King Celeus of Eleusis, who was nursed by Demeter and then dropped in the fire when she tried to make him immortal.
Dionysus	The god of wine, vegetation and the life-force, and of ecstasy. He was considered to be outside the Greek pantheon, and generally thought to have begun life as a mortal.
Dioscuri	Castor and Polydeuces, the twin sons of Zeus and Leda, who are important deities.
Dryads	Nymphs of the trees.
Echo	A nymph who was punished by Hera for her endless stories told to distract Hera from Zeus's infidelity.
Electra	Daughter of Agamemnon and Clytemnestra.
Eleusis	A town in which the cult of Demeter is centred.
Elpenor	The youngest of Odysseus's crew who fell from the roof of Circe's house on Aeaea and visited with Odysseus at Hades.
Elysium	The home of the blessed dead.
Eos	Goddess of the dawn and sister of the sun and moon.
Erichthonius	A child born of the semen spilled when Hephaestus tried to rape Athena on the Acropolis.
Eros	God of Love, the son of Aphrodite.
Erysichthon	A Thessalian who cut down a grove sacred to Demeter, who punished him with eternal hunger.
Eteocles	Son of Oedipus.
Eumaeus	Swineherd of Odysseus's family at Ithaca.
Euphemus	A son of Poseidon who could walk on water. He sailed with the Argonauts.
Europa	Daughter of King Agenor of Tyre, who was taken by Zeus to Crete.
Eurydice	A Thracian nymph married to Orpheus.
Fates	Daughters of Zeus and Themis, who spin the thread of a mortal's life and cut it when his time is due.
Furies	Creatures born from the blood of Cronus, guarding the greatest sinners of the Underworld. Their power lay in their ability to drive mortals mad. Snakes writhed in their hair and around their waists.
Gaea	Goddess of Earth, born from Chaos, and the mother of Uranus and Pontus.
Galatea	Daughter of Nereus and Doris, a sea-nymph loved by Polyphemus, the Cyclops.
Giants	A race of beings born from Gaea, grown from the blood that dropped from the castrated Uranus.
Golden Fleece	Fleece of the ram sent by Poseidon to substitute for Phrixus when his father was going to sacrifice him. The Argonauts went in search of the fleece.
Gorgon	One of the three sisters, including Medusa, whose frightening looks could turn mortals to stone.
Graces	Daughters of Aphrodite by Zeus.
Hades	One of the three sons of Cronus; brother of Poseidon and Zeus, who is King of the Underworld, known as the House of Hades.

Harmonia	Daughter of Ares and Aphrodite, wife of Cadmus.
Hector	Eldest son of King Priam who defended Troy from the Greeks. He was killed by Achilles.
Hecuba	The second wife of Priam, King of Troy. She was turned into a dog after Troy was lost.
Helen	Daughter of Leda and Tyndareus, King of Sparta, and the most beautiful woman in the world. She was responsible for starting the Trojan War.
Helius	The sun, son of Hyperion and Theia.
Hephaestus	Son of Zeus and Hera, god of fire and blacksmith of the gods.
Hera	A Mycenaean palace goddess, married to Zeus.
Heracles	An important Greek hero, the son of Zeus and Alcmena. His name means 'Glory of Hera'. He performed twelve labours for King Eurystheus, and later became a god.
Hermes	The conductor of souls of the dead to Hades, and god of trickery and of trade. He acts as messenger to the gods.
Hero and Leander	Hero was a priestess of Aphrodite, loved by Leander, a young man of Abydos. He drowned trying to see her.
Hestia	Goddess of the Hearth, daughter of Cronus and Rhea.
Hubris	Presumptuous behaviour which causes the wrath of the gods to be brought on to mortals.
Iambe	Daughter of Pan and Echo, servant to King Celeus of Eleusis and Metaeira.
Icarus	Son of Daedalus, who plunged to his death after escaping from the labyrinth.
Iphigenia	The eldest daughter of Agamemnon and Clytemnestra who was sacrificed to appease Artemis and obtain a fair wind for Troy.
Iris	Messenger of the gods who took the form of a rainbow.
Jason	Son of Aeson, King of Iolcus and leader of the voyage of the Argonauts.
Keres	Black-winged demons or daughters of the night.
Kore	'Maiden', another name for Persephone.
Labyrinth	A prison built at Knossos for the Minotaur by Daedalus.
Laertes	King of Ithaca and father of Odysseus.
Laestrygonians	Savage giants encountered by Odysseus on his travels.
Laocoon	A Trojan wiseman who predicted that the wooden horse contained Greek soldiers.
Laomedon	The King of Troy who hired Apollo and Poseidon to build the impregnable walls of Troy.
Leda	Daughter of the King of Aetolia, who married Tyndareus. Helen and Clytemnestra were her daughters.
Lethe	One of the four rivers of the Underworld, also called the River of Forgetfulness.
Lotus-Eaters	A race of people who live a dazed, drugged existence the result of eating the lotus flower.
Medea	Witch and priestess of Hecate, daughter of Aeetes and sister of Circe. She helped Jason in his quest for the Golden Fleece.
Medusa	One of the three Gorgons whose head had the power to turn onlookers to stone.
Melpomene	One of the muses, and mother of the Sirens.
Menelaus	King of Sparta, brother of Agamemnon. Married Helen and called war against Troy when she eloped with Paris.
Metaneira	Wife of Celeus, King of Eleusis, who hired Demeter in disguise as her nurse.
Minos	King of Crete, son of Zeus and Europa. He was considered to have been the ruler of a sea empire.
Minotaur	A creature born of the union between Pasiphae and a Cretan Bull.
Moly	A magical plant given to Odysseus by Hermes as protection against Circe's powers.
Muses	Goddesses of poetry and song, daughters of Zeus and Mnemosyne.
Narcissus	Son of the River Cephisus. He fell in love with himself and died as a result.
Nausicaa	Daughter of Alcinous, King of Phaeacia, who fell in love with Odysseus.

Nectar	Drink of the gods.
Nemesis	Goddess of retribution and daughter of night.
Neoptolemus	Son of Achilles and Deidameia, he came to Troy at the end of the war to wear his father's armour. He sacrificed Polyxena at the tomb of Achilles.
Nereids	Sea-nymphs who are the daughters of Nereus and Doris. Thetis, mother of Achilles, was a Nereid.
Nestor	Wise King of Pylus, who led the ships to Troy with Agamemnon and Menelaus.
Nymphs	Minor female deities associated with particular parts of the land and sea.
Odysseus	Greek hero, son of Laertes and Anticleia, who was renowned for his cunning, the master behind the victory at Troy, and known for his long voyage home.
Oedipus	Son of Leius, King of Thebes and Jocasta. Became King of Thebes and married his mother.
Olympia	Zeus's home in Elis.
Olympus	The highest mountain in Greece and the ancient home of the gods.
Oracle	The response of a god or priest to a request for advice – also a prophecy.
Orestes	Son of Agamemnon and Clytemnestra who escaped following Agamemnon's murder to King Strophius. He later returned to Argos to murder his mother and avenge the death of his father.
Orpheus	Thracian singer and poet, son of Oeagrus and a Muse. Married Eurydice and when she died tried to retrieve her from the Underworld.
Palamedes	Hero of Nauplia, inventor of the alphabet. He tricked Odysseus into joining the fleet setting out for Troy by placing the infant Telemachus in the path of his plough.
Palladium	Wooden image of Athene, created by her as a monument to her friend Pallas who she accidentally killed. While in Troy it protected the city from invaders.
Pallas	Athene's best friend, whom she killed.
Pan	God of Arcadia, half goat and half man. Son of Hermes. He is connected with fertility, masturbation and sexual drive. He is also associated with music, particularly his pipes, and with laughter.
Pandareus	Cretan King killed by the gods for stealing the shrine of Zeus.
Pandora	The first woman, created by the gods, to punish man for Prometheus's theft of fire. Her dowry was a box full of powerful evil.
Paris	Handsome son of Priam and Hecuba of Troy, who was left for dead on Mount Ida but raised by shepherds. Was reclaimed by his family, then brought them shame and caused the Trojan War by eloping with Helen.
Pegasus	The winged horse born from the severed neck of Medusa.
Peleus	Father of Achilles. He married Antigone, caused her death, and then became King of Phthia. Saved from death himself by Jason and the Argonauts. Married Thetis, a sea nymph.
Penelope	The long-suffering but equally clever wife of Odysseus who managed to keep at bay suitors who longed for Ithaca while Odysseus was at the Trojan War and on his ten-year voyage home.
Persephone	Daughter of Zeus and Demeter who was raped by Hades and forced to live in the Underworld as his queen for three months of every year.
Perseus	Son of Danae, who was made pregnant by Zeus. He fought the Gorgons and brought home the head of Medusa. He eventually founded the city of Mycenae and married Andromeda.
Phaeacia	The Kingdom of Alcinous on which Odysseus landed after a shipwreck which claimed the last of his men as he left Calypso's island.
Philoctetes	Malian hero, son of Poeas, received Heracles's bow and arrows as a gift when he lit the great hero's pyre on Mount Oeta. He was involved in the last part of the Trojan War, killing Paris.
Polyphemus	A Cyclopes, but a son of Poseidon. He fell in love with Galatea, but she spurned him. He was blinded by Odysseus.
Polyxena	Daughter of Priam and Hecuba of Troy. She was sacrificed on the grave of Achilles by Neoptolemus.
Poseidon	God of the sea, and of sweet waters. Also the god of earthquakes. His is brother to Zeus and Hades, who divided the earth between them.
Priam	King of Troy, married to Hecuba, who bore him Hector, Paris, Helenus, Cassandra, Polyxena, Deiphobus and

	Troilus. He was murdered by Neoptolemus.
Proetus	King of Argos, son of Abas.
Prometheus	A Titan, son of Iapetus and Themus. He was champion of mortal men, which he created from clay. He stole fire from the gods and was universally hated by them.
Proteus	The old man of the sea who watched Poseidon's seals.
Psyche	A beautiful nymph who was the secret wife of Eros, against the wishes of his mother Aphrodite, who sent Psyche to perform many tasks in hope of causing her death. She eventually married Eros and was allowed to become partly immortal.
Pygmalion	A sculptor who was so lonely he carved a statue of a beautiful woman, and eventually fell in love with it. Aphrodite brought the image to life.
Rhea	Mother of the Olympian gods. Cronus ate each of her children but she concealed Zeus and gave Cronus a swaddled rock in its place.
Scamander	River running across the Trojan plain, and father of Teucer.
Selene	Moon-goddess, daughter of Hyperion and Theia. She was seduced by Pan, but loved Endymion.
Sisyphus	King of Ephrya and a trickster who outwitted Autolycus. He was one of the greatest sinners in Hades.
Satyrs	Elemental spirits which took great pleasure in chasing nymphs. They had horns, a hairy body and cloven hooves.
Scylla and Charybdis	Scylla was a monster who lived on a rock of the same name in the Straits of Messina, devouring sailors. Charybdis was a whirlpool in the Straits which was supposedly inhabited by the hateful daughter of Poseidon.
Sirens	Sea nymphs who are half-bird, half-woman, whose song lures hapless sailors to their death.
Styx	River in Arcadia and one of the four rivers in the Underworld. Charon ferried dead souls across it into Hades, and Achilles was dipped into it to make him immortal.
Syrinx	An Arcadian nymph who was the object of Pan's love.
Tantalus	Son of Zeus who told the secrets of the gods to mortals and stole their nectar and ambrosia. He was condemned to eternal torture in Hades, where he was tempted by food and water but allowed to partake of neither.
Tartarus	Dark region, below Hades.
Telegonus	Son of Odysseus and Circe, who was allegedly responsible for his father's death.
Telemachus	Son of Odysseus and Penelope who was aided by Athene in helping his mother to keep away the suitors in Odysseus' absence.
Tereus	King of Daulis who married Procne, daughter of Pandion King of Athens. He fell in love with Philomela, raped her and cut out her tongue.
Thalia	Muse of pastoral poetry and comedy.
Theia	Goddess of many names, and mother of the sun.
Theseus	Son of King Aegeus of Athens. A cycle of legends has been woven around his travels and life.
Thetis	Chief of the Nereids loved by both Zeus and Poseidon. They married her to a mortal, Peleus, and their child was Achilles. She tried to make him immortal by dipping him in the River Styx.
Tiresias	A Theban who was given the gift of prophecy by Zeus. He was blinded for seeing Athene bathing. He continued to use his prophetic talents after his death, advising Odysseus.
Tisamenus	Son of Orestes, who inherited the Kingdom of Argos and Sparta.
Triton	A sea-god, and son of Poseidon and Amphitrite. He led the Argonauts to the sea from Lake Tritonis.
Trojan War	War waged by the Greeks against Troy, in order to reclaim Menelaus's wife Helen, who had eloped with the Trojan prince Paris. Many important heroes took part, and form the basis of many legends and myths.
Tyndareus	King of Sparta, perhaps the son of Perseus's daughter Grogphone. Expelled from Sparta but restored by Heracles. married Leda and fathered Helen and Clytemnestra, among others.
Xanthus & Balius	Horses of Achilles, immortal offspring of Zephyrus Balius the west wind. A gift to Achilles's father Peleus.
Zeus	King of gods, god of sky, weather, thunder, lightning, home, hearth and hospitality. He plays important role as the voice of justice, arbitrator between man and gods, and among them. Married to Hera, but lover of dozens of others.

Further Reading

Apollonius of Rhodes, *Jason and the Argonauts* (Penguin, 1995) • Garnett, L.M.J., *Greek Folk Tales* (Eliot Stock, 1885) • Grant, Michael, *Myths of the Greeks and Romans* (Michael Grant, 1989) • Graves, Robert, *The Greek Myths* (Penguin, 1955) • Grimal, Pierre, *The Dictionary of Classical Mythology* (Blackwell, 1986) • Hesiod, *The Homeric Hymns* (Loeb, 1914) • Homer, *The Iliad* (Loeb, 1928) • Homer, *The Odyssey* (Loeb, 1928) • Hope Moncrieff, A.R., *Classical Mythology* (George Harrap, 1907) • Kirk, G.S., *The Nature of Greek Myths* (Penguin, 1974) • Kirk, G.S., *Homer and the Oral Tradition* (Cambridge University Press, 1976) • Kupper, G.H., *The Legends of Greece and Rome* (O.C. Heath & Co., 1910) • Lang, A., *Homeric Hymns* (George Allen, 1899) • Morford, M.P.O., and Lenardon, R.J., *Classical Mythology* (Longman, 1985) • Otto, W.F., *The Homeric Gods: The Spiritual Significance of Greek Religion* (Thames and Hudson, 1955) • Petiseus, A.H., *The Gods of Olympus* (Fischer Unwin, 1892) • Seton-Williams, M.V., *Greek Legends and Stories* (Rubicon Press, 1993) • Sharwood Smith, John, and Johnson, Michael, *The Greeks and Their Myths* (Eurobook Limited, 1992) • Stoneman, Richard, *An Encyclopaedia of Myth and Legend: Greek Mythology* (Aquarian Press, 1991) • Warner, R., *Men and Gods* (Penguin, 1952) • Wood, Michael, *In Search of the Trojan War* (BBC Books, 1987)

Illustration Notes

Pages 2 *Bath of Psyche*, by Frederic Leighton (Tate Gallery, London). Courtesy of The Bridgeman Art Library. **Pages 5** *Nymphs Bathing by Classical Ruins*, by Abraham Van Cuylenborch (Johnny Van Haeften Gallery, London). Courtesy of The Bridgeman Art Library. **Pages 7** *Hermes, Herse & Aglauros*, by Veronese (Fitzwilliam Museum, University of Cambridge). Courtesy of the Visual Arts Library. **Pages 9** *Venus and Adonis*, by Jacopo Amigoni (Agnew & Sons, London). Courtesy of The Bridgeman Art Library. **Pages 11** *Landscape with the Father of Psyche Sacrificing to Apollo*, by Claude Lorrain (National Trust Fairhaven). Courtesy of The Bridgeman Art Library. **Pages 14** *Apollo and Marsyas*, by Pietro Perugino (Louvre, Paris). Courtesy of The Bridgeman Art Library. **Pages 17** *Minerva Visiting the Muses on Mount Helicon*, by Hans Jordaens III (Phillips, The International Fine Art Auctioneers). Courtesy of The Bridgeman Art Library. **Pages 19** *Poseidon and Amphitrite*, by Jacques de Gheyn II (Staatliche Museen Preuss. Kulturbesitz, W. Berlin). Courtesy of The Bridgeman Art Library. **Pages 21** *The Burning of Troy (panel)*, by Louis de Caullery (Galerie de Jonckheere, Paris). Courtesy of The Bridgeman Art Library. **Pages 29** *Venus and Mercury*, by Pierre-Nolasque Bergeret (Rafael Valls Gallery, London). Courtesy of The Bridgeman Art Library. **Pages 26** *The Abduction of Helen*, by Guido Reni (Louvre, Paris). Courtesy of Giraudon and The Bridgeman Art Library. **Pages 29** *The Siege of Troy*, by Rombout Van Troyen (Phillips, The International Fine Art Auctioneers). Courtesy of The Bridgeman Art Library. **Pages 31** *Ulysses Ploughing the Sea Shore*, by Heywood Hardy (David Messum Fine Paintings, Buckinghamshire). Courtesy of The Bridgeman Art Library. **Pages 33** *The Departure of Aeneas*, by Giuseppe Marchese (Phillips, The International Fine Art Auctioneers). Courtesy of The Bridgeman Art Library. **Pages 33** *Trojan Horse*, by Niccolo dell Abbate (Galleria Estense, Modena). Courtesy of The Bridgeman Art Library. **Pages 36** *The Burning of Troy*, by Pieter Schoubroeck (Phillips, The International Fine Art Auctioneers). Courtesy of The Bridgeman Art Library. **Pages 39** *The Sacrifice of Polyxena*, by G. B. Pittoni (Munich, Altepinakotiek). Courtesy of The Bridgeman Art Library. **Pages 41** *Aeneas and His Father Fleeing Troy*, by Simon Vouet (San, Diego, Museum of Art, USA). Courtesy of The Bridgeman Art Library. **Pages 45** *The Conversion of Ulysses*, by Hippolyte-Casimir Gourse (Whitford & Hughes, London). Courtesy of The Bridgeman Art Library. **Pages 47** *Landscape with the Arrival of Aeneas at Pallanteum*, by Claude Lorrain (National Trust, Anglesey Abbey). Courtesy of The Bridgeman Art Library. **Pages 49** *The Feast of Achelous*, by Rubens & Bruegel (Metropolitan, New York). Courtesy of The Visual Art Library. **Pages 53** *The Cyclops*, by Odilon Redon (Rijksmuseum Kroller-Muller, Otterlo). Courtesy of The Bridgeman Art Library. **Pages 57** *Landscape with Apollo Guarding the Herds of Admetus*, by Claude Lorrain (Palazzo Doria Pamphili, Rome). Courtesy of The Bridgeman Art Library. **Pages 58** *Circe Offering the Cup to Ulysses*, by John William Waterhouse (Oldham Art Gallery, Lancs). Courtesy of The Bridgeman Art Library. **Pages 61** *Circe and Ulysses*, by Camillo Paderni (Phillips, The International Fine Art Auctioneers). Courtesy of The Bridgeman Art Library. **Pages 63** *Circe*, by Wright Barker (Bradford City Art Gallery & Museums). Courtesy of The Bridgeman Art Library. **Pages 64** *Circe*, by Giovanni Castiglione (Galleria Degli Uffizi, Florence). Courtesy of The Bridgeman Art Library. **Pages 69** *The Sirens*, by Sir Edward Burne-Jones (National Gallery of South Africa, Cape Town). Courtesy of The Bridgeman Art Library. **Pages 70** *Ulysses and the Sirens*, by Herbert Draper (Ferens Art Gallery, Hull). Courtesy of The Bridgeman Art Library. **Pages 75** *A Fantastic Cave with Odysseus and Calypso*, Jan Brueghel (Johnny Van Haeften Gallery, London). Courtesy of The Bridgeman Art Library. **Pages 79** *Pallas and the Centaur*, by Sandro Botticelli (Galleria Degli Uffizi, Florence). Courtesy of The Bridgeman Art Library. **Pages 81** *Odysseus*, by Jacob Jordaens (Pushkin Museum, Moscow). Courtesy of The Bridgeman Art Library. **Pages 83** *Nausicaa and her Maidens playing at ball*, by Sir Edward John Poynter (Christie's, London). Courtesy of The Bridgeman Art Library. **Pages 85** *The Return of Ulysses*, by John Linnell (Forbes Magazine Collection, New York). Courtesy of The Bridgeman Art Library. **Pages 88** *Lesbia*, by John Reinhard Weguelin (Christie's London). Courtesy of The Bridgeman Art Library. **Pages 91** *Landscape: Aeneas at Delos*, by Claude Lorrain (National Gallery, London). Courtesy of The Bridgeman Art Library. **Pages 97** *Cupid and Psyche*, by Antonio Canova (Museo Correr, Venice). Courtesy of The Bridgeman Art Library. **Pages 101** *Ascent of Psyche to Olympus*, by Peter Paul Rubens (Meretown House, Roxburghshire). Courtesy of The Bridgeman Art Library. **Pages 105** *Persephone*, by Anthony Frederick Augustus Sandys (The Fine Art Society, London). Courtesy of The Bridgeman Art Library. **Pages 109** *Orpheus with Birds and Beasts*, by Roelandt Jacobsz Savery (Fitzwilliam Museum, University of Cambridge). Courtesy of The Bridgeman Art Library. **Pages 111** *Echo and Narcissus*, by Nicolas Poussin (Louvre, Paris). Courtesy of Giraudon and The Bridgeman Art Library. **Pages 113** *Narcissus*, by Umbrian School (City of Bristol, Museum & Art Gallery). Courtesy of The Bridgeman Art Library. **Pages 114** *Echo and Narcissus*, by John William Waterhouse (Walker Art Gallery, Liverpool). Courtesy of The Bridgeman Art Library. **Pages 117** *The Escape of Perseus*, by Sir Edward Burne-Jones (Southampton Art Gallery, Hampshire). Courtesy of the Bridgeman Art Library. **Pages 121** *Minotaur*, by George Frederick Watts (Tate Gallery, London). Courtesy of The Bridgeman Art Library. **Pages 125** *Jason Swearing Eternal Affection to Medea*, by Jean Francois de Troy (National Gallery, London). Courtesy of The Bridgeman Art Library.

Index